Magic, Spells & Potions
by StarFields

Magic, Spells & Potions

by StarFields

First Edition 2009

ISBN 978-1-873483-79-4

Published By

DragonRising Publishing

United Kingdom

Magic, Spells and Potions by StarFields

1st Edition Paperback

ISBN: 978-1-873483-79-4

DragonRising Publishing
45 Gildredge Road
Eastbourne
BN21 4RY
United Kingdom

Contact: staff@DragonRising.com / +44 (0)1323 700 123

Links:

- DragonRising Publishing: http://DragonRising.com/
- Magic, Spells & Potions: http://Magic-Spells-And-Potions.com/
- Silvia Hartmann: http://SilviaHartmann.com/

Table of Contents

Welcome To Magic, Spells & Potions 13

The Heart Of Magic 18
Magic & The Even Flow 22
The Target & Magical Certainty 26
Magic & Energy 30
Example: Strawberry Love Potion 34

New Symbols For A New Magic 37

Understanding The Genius Symbols 43
Working With The Symbols 46
Connecting With The Symbols 50
Clearing The Paths Exercise 53
Levels Of Magic Power 55
Magic Events 57
The Archer "Sunrise" Exercise 59
Feeling The Magic 63
Making An Art Solutions Energy Device Exercise 65
Practice Feeling The Magic 68
Attention & Energy Magic 70
Understanding Magic Failure 75
The Symbol Pantheon 80
The Gift 82
Receiving The Gift 85

The 23 Genius Symbols.. 87

Space...89
Time..91
Weather 93
The Land 95
The Crystal..97
The Plant 99
The Animal 101
The Human Being..103
The House..105
The Aspect 107
Magic 108
The Dance 109
The Alien..111
The Spirit..113
The Artefact 114
The Star 116
The Fountain 118
The Gift 120
The Trade 122
The Angel...124
The Friend..126
DragonWings 128
Star Dust..130
All Symbols 131
Your First Symbol Set..132
First Symbol Set Activation Ritual 134

Travel In The Magic Realms 137

The Classic Game 141
The Magical Self Within 151
Your Magic Central 152
The Magic Quest 153
Your Magic Name 154
Healing Domains 155
Meeting Helpful Spirits 156
Soul Piloting 157
The Magical Child Within 159
The Magical Demon Within 160
Spiritualism 162
Exploring Your Magical Heritage 164
Past Life Regression 165
Saving The Evil Magicians & Witches 167
The Classic Game In Overview 169

The Magic Of The Moment 171

Creating Magical Tools 175

The Magic Wand 178
Using The Magic Wand 180
Using The Energy Wand In Sanctuary 181
The Descendants Of The Magic Wand 183

Magic Stones 185

The Healing Stone Exercise 187
Making A Family Grid 189
Counting Your Blessings 192
The Descendants Of Stone Magic 194

Water Magic 197

Imprinting Water 200
Imprinting Water Using The Gift Exercise 203
Natural Healing Water 205

Fire Magic 207

Writing A Letter To The Powers That Be Exercise 210
Fire As The Symbol Of Magic 213
Single Candle Meditation Exercise 214
Candle Magic 215

Magic Words 217

The Magic Drum 220
The Magic Drum Exercise 220
Sound & Rhythm 222
Spirit Singing Exercise 222
Power Words & Magic 224
Rhyming Spells 226
A Little Rhyming Spell For Witches 227
Love Poem Exercise 230

The Magic Machine 231

No Reversed Symbols 234
The Basic Symbol Sphere 235
The Centre Of The Sphere 240
The Speed Of Magic 243
Powering Up The Sphere 245
Casting The Spell 249

The Silent Symbol Sphere 251

Choosing Specific Vibrations 255
The Focused Symbol Charging 257
Magic Perfume Exercise 259
The Symbol Wave 260
Symbol Sigils 262
Success Sigil For An Artist 263
Magic Circle Sigil 265
Sigil For Soul Protection 266
Protection Sigil For A House 267
A Sigil For ...? 269

Fortune Telling With The Genius Symbols 271

Magic As A Social Activity 275
A Simple Single Symbol Reading Example 279
The Three Symbol Reading 284
The Zodiac Reading 286
Reading Symbol Sentences 288

Fortune Telling By Magic Stories 291

Dream Interpretation By Magic Story 294

Spells & Potions 297

Mini-Spells or Spell Chants 300
Money Spell Chant 300
Anti-Stress Spell Chant 301
Spell Chant To Stop Panic In A Chaos Situation 302
Spell Chant To Bring A New Lover 303
Spell Chant For Making A Protection Sphere 304
Spell Chant For Starting A New Project 304
Spell Singing 305
Potions 307

A Potion For Family Prosperity 309
A Potion For A Sad Horse 311
A Potion To Re-Awaken Interest In A Husband 313

Spells & Rituals 315

Stone & Sea 317
A Simple Deliverance Spell 319
An Easy Distance Healing Spell 322
Safe Revenge Spell 324
Butterfly Spell For A New Future 328

Energy Creations 331

Riversmooth Shield & Glamour 334
Energy Artefacts 337
The Snow Globe 338
The Owl Feather 340
Silk Scarves & Cloaks 341
Energy Installations – Home & Garden 342
Energy Pets & Invisible Friends 345
Toy Poodle 345
Energy Familiars 346
The Wits 348
Friends 349
Hitchhikers 352
The Specialists 353

Farewell 357

Further Reading... 361

The Patterns & Techniques of EmoTrance by Silvia Hartmann 363
EmoTrance Energy Dancing by Silvia Hartmann 365
Project Sanctuary & The Genius Symbols 366
Fiction by StarFields 369
Improve Psychic Skills, Paranormal Abilities with Energy Hypnosis 371
The Aromatherapy Collection 372
HypnoDreams & Energy Hypnosis 374
Healing & Affirmations 376

WELCOME TO MAGIC, SPELLS & POTIONS

As I was writing this book, it became more and more clear to me that true magic has its own way of protecting itself against being abused by the wrong kinds of people.

Real magic is surprisingly simple.

There is nothing spooky about it, and instead, it is completely amazing, joyful and so enriching, it's simply extraordinary on every level.

That being so, I kept asking myself WHY?

WHY are there all these mountains of misleading, contradictory, misguided, labyrinthine, bizarre, illogical, confusing, simply WEIRD information about magic?

WHY are there such peculiar, unnatural systems being proposed, and studied, and practised by likewise, very peculiar people across the ages?

It may be so that this happens as magic protects itself against people who can't feel it, don't know what it is, and at the end of the day, DON'T ACTUALLY WANT TO KNOW WHAT IT IS OR HOW IT WORKS because they're much happier playing some kind of weird mind game with themselves and each other, in order to avoid change and keep themselves busy for decades, or a whole life long.

Perhaps in order to be able to enter the true heart of magic, one has to be able to walk through that labyrinth of nonsense without fear, without letting oneself being side tracked by all these mutterings of the ages, and let the heart lead the way.

Perhaps only those who are really TRUE OF HEART and want to know magic for its own sake get to make their way through the labyrinth, and not those out to "get rich quick" or "get power over other people" or "get laid" or any of those reasons that attracts the wrong crowd to the practice of magic.

That would certainly preclude true magic ever falling into the hands of the wrong people - and it seems to me, that's worked pretty well across the ages.

Now is a new age.

Now is a good time to start afresh with magic, look at it through new eyes, as they say look at it "with the eyes of a child" and that's the way to get through the labyrinth and reach the real heart of magic.

I have written this book not for those who are already set in their ways and comfortable in their forms of whatever magic they practice, but for those who want to learn something about the true nature of magic, by picking up their power to question, to experiment, and to start a real relationship with magic - and to use it to enrich their lives in a way that nothing else ever could.

There is a wonderful freedom in magic, a wonderful expression of self and one's love for the Universe, given and received; there is joy and delight of the highest order, a lightness and a beauty above all else that reflects the awesome Creative Order itself.

I personally believe that it is our magic that makes us really human, and really quite special, and surely extra-blessed by the Creator who gave us these talents, skills, and possibilities.

This book might not be the last word on magic, but for some amongst you it will be the first word, an introduction and a guide, firstly back to yourself and from there, out into the Universe at large where there is so much fun, excitement, challenge, endeavour, success and surprising gifts awaiting us all - at least all of those amongst us who truly want to find the heart of magic.

StarFields

Anno 2009

The Heart Of Magic

Magic is the science of change.

Unlike many other human past times, magic is not a spectator sport.

Magic is active; it is always essentially taking action in order to make changes in the world.

In that way, magic is like an arrow. You can't see the results until and unless the target has been hit; then the results are abundantly clear and appear "just like magic". If you don't hit the target and the arrow disappears into the blue sky, or into the forest, or falls into the lake it may seem that for a lot of work nothing has happened at all.

- **It is this feature of magic, namely that either you've hit the target and there is massive change on all levels, or you don't, and nothing**

seems to have happened at all, that makes magic difficult for beginners.

In this on-off results set, there aren't any "near misses".

There isn't any "it works a little bit, and if I keep at it, it'll work a little bit more" to guide you in the cold, cool, warm, hot! version of learning how to do magic.

Magic either works - or it doesn't. On or Off.

For beginners, that's a double challenge.

Their first attempts are not going to work and it seems like nothing is happening at all; and that's like trying to learn to play the piano but it is entirely silent UNLESS YOU HIT THE CHORDS PERFECTLY - because only then, they will sound.

That's very demotivating and the amount of people who "tried" to study magic, got no results, and gave up shortly after, is legion.

The other part of the challenge is that when magic does work, people are so shocked by this, they get scared - and give up magic shortly after as well!

In that way, magic functions as a filter to itself. Magic takes out those who don't have what it takes to do magic by virtue of its own design.

To keep persevering with magic even when you don't get any noticeable results at all, and then, to stay strong and remain unafraid when it does work all of a sudden, you need to have magic in your heart.

You need to not just "believe in magic".

- **You need to know that magic is real.**

You need to know that in your mind, and feel it in your body.

Until and unless you do, you won't succeed in the study of magic, indeed, you can't succeed.

But take heart.

When we let go of our fears and disappointments, prejudices and old wife's tails and all the nonsense and propaganda of the ages, and we step towards magic fresh and young, like children would, it reveals itself to us.

We are all magical beings, living in a magical universe.

We are born that way; we are born into a magical universe of which we are a part.

All that stands between magic being delightful and as useful as coming across an orchard full of delicious nutritious fruit in the middle of the forest, is our fears, our misconceptions, and the propaganda of the ages.

These fears and misconceptions cause our hands to shake when we fire the arrow of magic from the bow of our intention and desire; that is what causes the targets to be missed, the arrows to disappear into the blue yonder and the misunderstanding that "magic doesn't work" or that "magic doesn't work FOR ME".

Magic does work. Magic is perfectly real. Magic is very logical. Magic is even quite simple.

Magic is also delightful, and LIGHT in nature; and there again, all those swirling fears and misconceptions, medieval thinking and general misery of the ages has played havoc with the proper expression and experience of magic.

When you can recover the lightness and the joy of magic, learning it like a child would, with curiosity and delight in the truest sense of the word, and you approach magic like that, it will gladly open the doors and invite you in.

Magic will show you a world of potential, possibility and true beauty; a place where you are not and never alone, where there are friends, helpers, guides on many different levels; and where you as one individual person have all the skills, talents and abilities necessary to thrive and live a good life.

- **Remember: Magic is light, and beautiful. If you ever lose that, you have lost the heart of magic.**

Magic & The Even Flow

Imagine you are standing in a clearing with your bow and arrow, and your target some distance away.

Imagine that you breathe cleanly; that you raise the bow and arrow smoothly and in confidence, aligning yourself with the target.

You pay attention to the target, for your attention will become the road upon which the arrow will travel; and all that is so smooth and flowing, that an observer wouldn't see a single break or stoppage in the movement as you raise the bow and raise your head and then release the arrow - proudly it flies, swiftly it flies on the prescribed path and hits the target dead centre.

You lower the bow, and you bow your head with a swift smile.

This is how it's done.

This is the only way to do it.

You may have spent many weeks or even months making the bow, making the arrows. You may have travelled quite a distance to find the clearing in the forest, find the target and it may have taken you some time to decide when the right time would come to take your shot.

But that is preparation; in the end it comes down to that smooth movement, that time when all questions have been answered, all reservations laid aside, and now there is only you and the target and that arrow that flies straight to the heart of the target on your command as you simply release the tension in the bow.

That is how magic spells work; that is the model I want you to remember.

If ever you stray from that model, the archer in the clearing will take you back to how it is supposed to be.

There is a time of preparation; a time of stepping up to take the shot; there is the raising of the energy as we draw back the bow; and that focus of attention on the target that guides the arrow as we release this built up energy with force, and let the arrow go.

There is a smooth flow and an elegance to this which you need to pay attention to; for anything that disrupts the smooth flowing of the process overall will make the arrow become unstable; twist and turn in flight, and then there is every chance that it won't reach the target or that the arrow will become lost in the forest behind the target.

If we look at the archer, we can tell what kind of things would cause the even flow to be disrupted.

You know, and you don't have to be either a great magician, or a great physician to understand what kind of things will make quite sure that this archer will succeed, or fail.

If their hands are shaking with fear, they will fail.

If their thoughts are all over the place, thinking about this, that and the other, they will fail.

If their breathing is irregular, if their muscles are locked up tight with stress, they will fail.

If they're not sure if they are doing the right thing by hitting the target and are dithering, raising and lowering the bow repeatedly, you know it's not going to be a good clean shot in the end.

If their arrows are crooked and the bow is bent, of course, they will fail.

And finally, if they step up with the attitude of, "Oh what's the point ..." or "I'll give it a shot but ..." you can look at them and even before they've taken the shot, you can make a safe bet that they will fail.

That's you, that's me, that's anyone and everyone who tries to do magic.

- **You can't do magic when you're not flowing smoothly, when you're not calm, relaxed, and perfectly focused on the object of your magic change intervention.**

There is one more very important thing that will make our archer fail for sure - and that is when they can't even see the target!

The Target & Magical Certainty

Magic is about change.

We need to really deeply and profoundly know what we're doing, and most of all, **what we are trying to achieve**, before we set out to do the spell, create the ritual, make the potion, call in the specialist and instruct the higher forces.

You really need to be clear where and what your target is, what you want to achieve before you start.

Apart from stress and confusion putting a spoke into the smoothly rolling wheel of magic, being unclear about the target is the No. 1 reason for magic failure.

People have very nebulous ideas about what "getting rich" or "getting with Peter" or "getting healthy" or "winning this court case" might entail.

- **For magic to work as it should, you need a clear, powerful target that stands resonantly so our archer can see it, and aim for it, and hit it.**

You need a single, powerful vision that describes your aim and outcome, and that holds true from a little mundane every day spell to a great big piece of change work that involves centuries, continents, hundreds of thousands of people or more.

To create this magic target is in and of itself, a powerful magical skill; and if you do this right then **the target becomes so attractive** that it will literally draw the arrow of your magic work towards itself, as much as you build up energy from your end to release your intention.

That gives a "**double velocity**" which makes such a piece of magic work more powerful than just the sum of its parts; here, you could say we really create an impact on reality itself, and this is where real magic happens.

As before, you can't create such a resonant target when you are stressed and your thoughts, emotions and energies are jumping around all over the place.

You can't do it when you're in "two minds" about something - you have to be certain, you have to have reached **magical certainty about the rightness** of unleashing your arrow towards the target.

- **Magical certainty is the most powerful tool a practitioner of magic has.**

Magical certainty is a challenge as well as a protective

device. If you're not certain, your magic won't work and you are protected from outcomes that some aspects of you might think are a good idea but other aspects resist.

These aspects may be just simple human ones, but they can also be aspects from another source, such as your soul, or a guardian angel, who is putting uncertainty into your plans so they cannot come to pass, because they might not be in your best interest in the long run.

Magical certainty is thereby precious, and to reach it **before** you unleash the arrow is at least 50% of the workings of your magic.

With magical certainty also comes confidence, and alignment; the energy you raise when you are aligned is as powerful as a laser is in comparison to a hand held torch; and the difference that allows the laser to cut through steel and be visible from the moon is the perfect alignment of frequency to a single powerful intention.

The process a magician goes through to reach magical certainty is highly personal and it is one of the master keys to making magic your own, and discovering just how magical you really are.

In this book, you will learn a multitude of different ways to seek advice, to set better targets, to understand yourself better, and to get to a point where reaching magical certainty isn't some kind of major quest, but something you can work out quickly, and smoothly.

To sum up what I've told you here:

- **Remember the archer in the forest clearing in all your magical works. This is a model that can show you where you are not ready, and to make sure that you are before you take your shot and cast that spell.**
- **Learn about your stress levels, and learn to deal with those so that you can enter into a state of clarity and even flow before you set the target and raise the energy.**
- **Set the target clearly and cleanly, with magical certainty.**
- **Always remember that magic is light, joyous and beautiful. Do not proceed until you are clear about this because that tells you that you are in the right state, in the right place mentally, emotionally and spiritually to do magic, and to do it well.**

With these things in place, you are already in a better position to create pure, clean and powerful magic than 99% of those who profess to practice magic at this time.

Magic & Energy

In order to understand magic and work it correctly, we have to understand that the world is made up of some hard components, and these are the tips of the iceberg of much larger structures, which are the energy worlds.

Our icebergs also float in oceans of energy, on energy worlds, which exist within giant energy solar systems, and those are parts of even greater energetic galaxies, which swirl in the even greater context of the entire Universe.

All things have an energy component, and in order to work with real reality which is the hard plus the energy dimensions correctly, we need to first of all, **read the energetic realities behind the scenes of material objects**, and then put them together in such a way that we achieve a form of cocktail that does what we want it to do.

- **No-one can become a proper practitioner of magic, or ever do any real magic, if they cannot read and understand energetic realities.**

Such a person is energy blind and they will try to make up for this by using recipes from a spell book, copying out ideas and symbols and meanings that other people who were not so afflicted worked out and wrote down.

However, this doesn't help; someone without taste buds can't cook well, even if you give them the best recipe books of the ages, the best cookers and pots, and the best ingredients, they will NEVER become a master chef.

Worse, their food will never even taste good enough for a simple family dinner – and how could it?

The good news is that actually only very few people are really energy blind; most just simply haven't opened their eyes of night, as we call them, to take a good long look at the real energy dimensions of everything.

As always, 99% of that is fear - there is a lot of

information in the energy dimensions, and when all of a sudden someone is presented with view of the world where everything is alive, everything moves and shifts and there is a million times more going on at any given time than they ever suspected there was, a person can easily freak out and reflexively shut down their eyes of night, "This is too much! I'm scared! I don't want to know that much ..." style.

The fact is that this enormous amount of information about the energy worlds needs to be processed not by our conscious mind, but by our energy mind, which is a part of every person's energy body.

In order to do magic properly, we need to access the energy mind and use it to give us information about the world, and tell what we need to do in order to make changes there, taking EVERYTHING into consideration.

The energy mind doesn't work with "thoughts" or "words" but instead, works with visions.

Visions are not just what you see, but like a lucid dream, they have information that you feel through your energy body, hear through your other ears, see through your eyes of night and it all feels very real, much more than three dimensional, and fully autogenic.

For a practitioner of magic, the ability to step into visions is the first order of the day.

Once this becomes successfully achieved, everything else is a piece of cake, quite literally.

The energy mind is the gateway to the higher powers of the Universe, to one's own soul and higher aspects; and to the real information about the world around us.

Once we open this gateway, we gain access to premium information that we can use in our magic to make it safe and powerful in every way.

This premium information includes guidance and wisdom from ancestors and higher beings; it includes recipes for spells, instructions for rituals, information about how to make potions and charms, and is in essence our own personal book not of shadows, but of wondrous light filled existence, that is already written, already there, and all we have to do is to open it, and step inside.

Here is an example to make it clear what I mean by this.

Example: Strawberry Love Potion

I was asked to make a love potion for a girl called Gemma so that she would find the right love for her at this time.

I found myself standing in a field of strawberries in early summer; and so the first ingredient for the potion was strawberries.

I looked around and not far from the edge of the field, I could hear there was a colony of bees; so the second ingredient for the potion was honey.

Then a child came dancing by; she was delighted and wearing a white dress, pink ribbons in her hair.

So I knew that the potion, made from strawberries and honey, would be put into a clear bottle with a pink ribbon around the bottle's neck.

I asked if there was anything else, and my attention was drawn to a single drop of dew that lay on one of the leaves of the strawberry plants at my feet.

That was the last ingredient, the catalyst for the potion - a single drop of morning dew.

Perfect!

And what a beautiful potion for Gemma.

It took perhaps half a second to see all that and work it out; perhaps a second, at a stretch.

This potion is perfect for Gemma. It didn't come from a book in the library, it came from the energy mind who produced the vision; and in fact, with a little help from some angels and some fairies too that I noted with a smile where keeping an eye on the little girl in the white dress.

By following the simple and straightforward advice and methods in this book, you too will be able to have such visions and create perfect spells and potions for whoever might need your services.

If you are more interested in highly esoteric magic, rest assured that instead of a vision of a simple field of strawberries, you can go to places in time and space where you will stand in the middle of the most complex symbological mandalas you could ever imagine just the same.

As the energy mind stands in connection with the rest of the energy Universe, which includes all the unseen forces, powerful spirits, deities, natural energy forms and so much more besides, you are not alone and there is plenty of help available along the way.

In the meantime, I would like you to note that:

- **You have an energy mind,**
- **And that you can learn to access it easily, at will, any time and any where,**
- **And that through your visions, you will be able to receive the information you need,**
- **And the support you need, to make your magic work -**
- **And to make your magic beautiful, powerful, resonant and strong.**

New Symbols For A New Magic

This book on magic is for modern people, living in the modern world.

We have learned much since the days of what I call medieval thinking about how people work, how the world works; and probably the most important learning of all is how stress makes people stupid.

The more stressed a person becomes, the more crazy their thinking becomes in a direct cause and effect relationship; if you beat someone hard and long enough mentally, emotionally and spiritually, they will ALL begin to hallucinate a Universe filled with evil, pain, suffering and satanic demons at every step.

This is what happened in the Dark Ages - people were stressed to insanity by their brutal living conditions and the world around them, and they created brutal, horrendous forms of magic as a result that is filled to the brim with the ravings of schizophrenics which were mistaken for prophets in all that insanity.

From that time, we have inherited all manner of bizarre symbols and a magic idea that is terrifying, scary to the extreme, and laden with the energies of torturing witches, hell, demons, damnation, Satan itself.

Personally I have the saying, "I keep looking for Satan and all I find is crazy men."

It is time now to draw a line under all of that, and to look forward into a different future, one where people think clearly, feel cleanly, and begin to appreciate the true wonder of the Universe and all it holds.

This is a different world view from the medieval days;

and I would like you to note that we do not close our eyes to suffering, or wrong doing; or pretend that it's all about dancing bunny rabbits and happy-happy fairies.

To do that is to disrespect the divine Wilderness of the true Universe just as deeply in its own way as to pretend it is all suffering and evil.

- **The Universe is more than we can ever imagine, than we can ever know.**

There are certainly places that are dangerous to people's life and limb; there are certainly beings that are best avoided.

But you cannot live in a beautiful forest and spend all your time shivering under a tree for fear of wolves and bears, and lakes in which you may drown.

That would be no life, and there would be no justice done to that amazing world that is designed around us, as we are designed to live within it; if we stop freaking out and going crazy with stress and fear, and instead, we get up, step out into the sunlight and **PAY ATTENTION** to what there is, we can live here not just successfully, but spectacularly so.

So the time has come for new symbols, for a new magic, one that is respectful but also light and celebrates life in a very profound and basic way.

This is a magic that is natural to human beings, no matter who or when or where they are; men and women alike, all races, all civilisations, no exceptions.

Each person has their own life, their own viewpoint and their own experiences; so there is no "tour bus" to magic land.

To begin the study of magic for real, and that has to be done in a playful and light hearted way, like a child would explore their world, given room but kept safe and guided by the elders and the angels, each person must find their own path, their own way.

Each person must find their own spells, their own rituals, their own symbols, in the end.

Magic is for real people, not for sheep who can't think for themselves, who don't know how to feel unless they're told what to feel, and who can't or won't see what is really there.

If you are one of those, and you are ready and willing to make contact with first of all, your own energy mind, and through your energy mind, with the greater realities of our worlds and lives, all is ready and awaiting you.

In order to aid you in this highly personal endeavour, I have created a set of symbols to get us started, because I know how to touch the energy mind, and how to get it to respond to us.

These symbols are gateways; in and of themselves, they have no meaning other than that they are doorways to different lands where you get to have your own experiences, your own learnings, and where you get to make your own spells and discover your own magic, which is absolutely your own magic, and no-one else's.

I have stripped these new symbols of all forms of fear and evil and I have made it so that by using these symbols, **you will get support, and friendly help from the first time you touch them.**

These 23 symbols are stepping stones into the world of magic in a fresh, new, and personal way for intelligent people acting in the 21st century.

There is so much joy in real magic, so much hope and also, so much power to make our lives and that of others richer, more resonant, more beautiful, more purposeful and, in the end, celebrate life in the one true Universe in a whole new way.

So let us get started now, meet the symbols, and start getting that which we want out of magic, which is a level of control, and how to use the forces of the living Universe, visible and invisible, material and immaterial, to make our way in the world.

Understanding The Genius Symbols

These symbols are called The Genius Symbols because it is known that in order to be a genius, you need to be able to have visions.

- **The Genius Symbols induce visions. That is their purpose.**

These symbols are magical in every definition of the word.

If we compare the Genius Symbols to Tarot Cards, for example, you will notice that any single Tarot Card contain a multitude of mixed together symbology.

There are references and symbols from astrology, deities from a variety of different pantheons; there are numerology symbols, metaphors, iconography; the quarters are in there somewhere as well, and so on and so forth.

Any Tarot card is a cocktail of symbols from a variety of different magical systems that have accumulated for a long time; when you look at the Genius Symbols, you will notice that **each one only deals with one single energy form.**

This one energy form may exist on many levels, and as you mix and match the symbols you can get infinite combinations; but the important fact to remember is that each symbol stands for a single cohesive and congruent energy form.

When we interact with any one symbol, it functions like a portal that connects us DIRECTLY to the realm of that energy form.

As a simple example, here is the plant symbol.

When we make contact with that, we make contact with the green, the spirit of green life that underlies all other beings on Earth and is the basis for all life on Earth.

The Plant Kingdom is the oldest of all living kingdoms and in this kingdom, life as we know it began billions of years ago; and even though we people have evolved and became animals, then sentients, we still carry the Plant Kingdom in the deepest fibre of our beings.

We are linked to all life on Earth, have a communality amongst us, and when we pick up the Plant symbol, we touch that, step into that, are reminded of that, and can find our way to where that energy field of living green resides.

So it is important to understand that the symbol in and of itself is not the power; it is a connector that makes the bridge between us who are using the symbol, and that powerful energy form, energy universe that lies on the other side.

In our example of the Plant Kingdom, there may come a time when we need to address the Plant Kingdom as a whole - that includes the consciousness of the Plant Kingdom, the spirit (or God) of all plants; it includes not just plants that have already been, and that are here with us now, but also those still to come until the end of time.

This is very global, but within that we can become very specific.

We can say for example, "Show me one particular herb that I have growing in my garden that will heal my headache today."

We can use the Plant Symbol to access that information field of all plants and there we can find out which plant that lives in your garden can cure your headache today.

This shows you the range of what you can do with these symbols.

You can move all the way from the most mundane little practical uses, such as finding a herb for your headache on this day, to the most global, abstract, powerful, multidimensional computations that involve the spirit and consciousness of all plants through time and space elegantly and easily, using a single symbol.

We will learn how to direct at which level we want to work at as we go along; here, it is important for you to remember that every one of the Genius Symbols is such a portal as the Plant Symbol for the Plant Kingdom, to a field of information and existence that contains all the knowledge of that kingdom across time and space; and all 23 together, it has been said, describe the Universe.

Working With The Symbols

Working with the entire set of all 23 symbols does mean that you will have to understand each symbol on a personal level.

However, it doesn't mean you have to know them already before we even start.

- **In the act of playing with and working with the symbols, we get to know them better, and every time we use them, our understanding of the realms behind the doorways of those symbols grows, and so does our magic.**

You don't have to "fully understand" the plant symbol in order to take it out into the garden and have it show you to a plant that can cure your backache, headache, sadness on this day.

Just with that one symbol, and the most basic of first understandings what it is about and how it works, a whole wealth of opportunity to make healing and rejuvenating potions, charms and recipes through and from the Plant Kingdom reveals itself. Please do bear in mind that you might not want to eat the plant, or drink the potion; you might work with that plant's energy exclusively instead; but these finer points too will be revealed in due course.

I would like you to note that this one symbol, that of the Plant Kingdom, already represents MAJOR

MAGIC, and you haven't studied for dozens of years, you didn't have to remember by rote all sorts of rules and regulations, and in fact, you can get started exploring that Plant Kingdom right here and now, and gain benefits already from doing so.

ALL THE SYMBOLS ARE LIKE THAT.

They all structurally work in the same way, and I would like you to take a moment and reflect on what kind of DIRECT AND AWESOME power that already represents - and you haven't even begun to practice and experiment!

Of course, we don't just use one symbol by itself most of the time. The symbols can be used in patterns and combinations; and the most powerful form happens when they all work together in a Symbol Sphere that activates them all.

This is extremely powerful stuff and so it is important to remember that although we do have these symbols of a plant, or a crystal, a friend or an angel, the symbols themselves are not where it is at, but they are doorways.

And it matters not if you paint them into the air with your finger tip, or with a magic wand if you prefer, or you draw them onto a piece of card, a rock or a pretty piece of glass, THE SYMBOLS EXIST INDEPENDENTLY of whatever you put them on, and they always function as doorways, as portals, for two way traffic with the energy form they describe.

For example, now that you know the Plant symbol, you

can, for the rest of your life, and wherever you go, draw that symbol in order to open the portal to the Plant Kingdom, reliably and readily, and travel there, or channel energies and information from there.

You could draw this symbol onto your back door, the one that leads into your garden, and as you step through the door, you step not just physically into a physical garden, but into your personal Plant Kingdom, you could say, your personal temple to the spirit of plants.

You can draw the Plant symbol with your fingertip onto a cup that contains herbal tea and evoke the full energetic power of what now becomes a magic potion through your intention, opening the portal, and through the symbol, channelling the power of the Plant kingdom into this simple cup containing this simple tea.

You can draw the Plant symbol into the air to bless a landscape that needs the power of the Plant Kingdom to come to its rescue; and if someone is sick, you can evoke the Plant Kingdom for them so that on that level, they may be healed by the power of green.

So remember: Any of the 23 symbols exists independently of any object you might put them on, and you can put them on any object, person or existence you feel needs that connection, that energy form to come to their aid.

The more you understand each symbol, and the more closely you are personally connected through the symbol to the realm for which it stands, the more powerful and impressive your results are going to be.

Not only that, but as you learn to have these energies flow through you then you will find that this feels FANTASTIC, wonderful; it makes you feel alive, it makes you happy and it heals you in all sorts of amazing ways. It gives you wings.

The first step on this journey is to familiarise ourselves with the 23 symbols, and to make our first symbol set so we can start to learn more about the symbols and the energy forms they stand for, as well as being able to start USING the symbols in our magic right away.

Connecting With The Symbols

One of the truly wonderful aspects of the Genius Symbols is the fact that they are so easy to learn.

You do not have to wrap your mind around painful and alien concepts, letters, numbers and ideas; the symbols are natural and understood easily **by your conscious mind and by your energy mind.**

If we look at all 23 for a moment, you will notice that there are certain symbols you may have come to expect but they are not there.

There is no symbol for death, and no symbol for evil; there is no symbol for judgement, and there are no swords or other implements of war, no knives nor anything that could stab or hurt a person.

This is because all those concepts are people ideas; the symbols, on the other hand, don't deal with people ideas but with the basic concepts of the REAL living Universe, and all of those are entirely beyond judgement, and beyond fear or doubt.

- **These energy forms are all "innocent energies" - the symbols are neither good nor bad, they simply are, as are all things in nature.**

If you notice, all you have to do to make people become scared, stressed and unsure of themselves and the Universe around them, is to put a few demons and devils into a system of magic.

Remember our archer in the forest. If their hands start to shake in fear, their bodies start to quake in fear, their stomachs churn with fear and their minds go crazy with wild imaginings, they can NEVER HIT THE TARGET.

- **For all workings of magic it is of the ESSENCE that you should remain unafraid, and lightly buoyant, even joyful in your expectation of success and having a good experience, while we're there.**

Even with the absence of "demons and devils" it may be possible that some people are going to experience fear and stress with some of the symbols.

For example, someone who was once trampled by a horse may react negatively to the Animal symbol; some people might be afraid of the symbol that has the picture of a little ghost on it and denotes the spirit world.

Some people might look at the People symbol and reject it because they were hurt by people; some people might think they don't need the Trade symbol because they're not double glazing salespeople by profession and so it is irrelevant to them.

How anyone responds to the "innocent energies" of the symbols is highly idiosyncratic, that means it depends on the person and their life's experiences as to how exactly they are going to think and feel when they touch the energy of the symbols

Everybody is different, and there is nothing wrong with having all kinds of different emotional and energetic responses to each one of the symbols – in fact, it's completely natural, human and right that you should.

What you need to do however in order to work successfully especially with combinations of the symbols, and the powerful symbol spheres in particular, is to **take out those barriers that preclude a clean relationship with any of the symbols.**

Any mental, emotional or energetic block, confusion, fog or fear lying between you and the symbol will block the flow of energy from that realm and HINDER YOUR PROGRESS.

There are many simple ways in which to "clean up" your connection to the symbol, and then to make a straight path for you to travel on, through the symbol and into the realm for which the symbol is the doorway.

Here is the "Clearing The Paths Exercise".

Clearing The Paths Exercise

1. Place one single symbol in front of you.
2. Feel the energy form behind the symbol, let it come to you.
3. Can you feel it in your body? The ideal flow is that the energy should enter you, flow through you sweetly and smoothly, flow out and leave you refreshed and clean, very clear, very logical and powerfully balanced, ready for action.

   If this is not the case, is there firstly a shield to the symbol?

   Feel for it with your hands. This shield is made from energy and it will disappear if you use your hands of energy, your magical power hands if you will, to swirl or wipe the shield away.

   This swirling stuff that gets between you and the symbol is usually the entrainment we spoke of earlier, the old wife's tails and all of that nonsense that is like smog, stifling clear sight (clairvoyance!), stifling clear sounds (clairaudience!) and visions. It is immaterial, just dirt, and you can wipe it away and feel much better for it.
4. If you can feel the symbol energy in your body but it hurts, feels uncomfortable, or as though it

is striking a blockage inside your body, place your hands of magic (healing hands) onto that place with a healing intention and tell those energy forms there to "Soften and flow!"

You will feel the blockages to dissolve and the energy from the symbol can start to flow through you. Continue until the flow is powerful, crystal clear and really makes you feel alive.

This "clearing the paths" exercise is very powerful, very personal and it will also help you in the future to not get hurt or traumatized by magical energies that you will raise; those pathways through which the symbols energies travel are the pathways of magic energy in YOUR systems.

To have them clear and bright is wonderful for your mental, emotional and spiritual health and allows you to tackle problems with magic that would have made magicians of old who did not clear their paths successfully FIRST run and hide in fear of pain and suffering.

Also remember this exercise when you journey in these other places, other realms and other dimensions to bring back information for spells and rituals.

When you come across anything that causes you to feel pain in your body or causes emotional disturbances - CLEAR THE PATHS. This will save you much trouble, stop you from acting with "stress stupidity" and it will keep you safe even and sound on all levels and all layers.

Levels Of Magic Power

The symbols can reveal only what we can "take in" safely at this time; and likewise, the amount of power you can channel through the symbols and yourself is dependent on your experience, knowledge and wisdom.

This has two effects.

The first is that you are always comfortable with the symbols because they will act at the level you are at; this will keep you safe by definition.

The second is that as your magic power increases, so do the symbols power up at the same time.

With every time you use them, you learn more, and this sets up a developmental spiral taking your magic powers and your understanding of how magic works up, and up, and up.

Don't make the mistake to think that because the Genius Symbols are simple that they are not immeasurably powerful.

It is BECAUSE THEY ARE SIMPLE that they are so powerful.

The more complicated and confused you make anything, the less fruitful it becomes; the more frustrating, and the less the results for ever more effort expended.

If you are used to working with incredibly convoluted labyrinthine systems of magic, the sheer simplicity and elegance of the Genius Symbols takes a little getting used to, as do the extremely powerful energy forms in singular alignment that are channelled through the symbols.

Please use the "Clearing The Paths" exercise to have a logical, clean, clear relationship with the symbols so they can help you channel more and more profound insights, more powerful energy forms, and grow as both as a magician, but also as a human being.

Magic Events

Every spell, every ritual, every chant and every magic endeavour has at the very core of itself the "magic event" - that means that split second which may be no time at all when the arrow hits the target and the change in reality becomes manifest.

Every piece of magic needs an event to make it work.

This means that something happens that you can feel like a strike of lightning in your whole body, in your mind, in your energy system and YOU KNOW YOU HAVE CHANGED REALITY.

All the preparation beforehand and all time spent – long or short – in getting ready for the ritual is all designed only, and ONLY, to enable that magic event.

It sounds complicated, but it is simple enough – you know you got it right, you hit the target, and your spell will work when you have felt that lightning strike that ONLY happens when magic becomes manifest, and you really have changed the world.

Longer and more complicated spells and rituals may have a number of smaller events that are like a staircase leading up to the main event – the target, the purpose of the spell.

If you feel nothing, then nothing is happening.

That's incredibly simple and helps us to know when we

are making a spell that works, as opposed to when we don't.

- **Remember: The spell is about creating an event.**

In order to create this change event, we have already learned that we need the double velocity of the attraction of the target (the purpose of the spell) and the release of energy that is directed towards the target, in our metaphor the pulling back of the bow which RAISES THE ENERGY NEEDED TO PROPEL THE ARROW FORWARD towards the target.

The Archer "Sunrise" Exercise

1. Think of someone you would like to send some golden sunshine energy to, as a magic gift and for practice purposes.[1] Be sure that all parts of you agree on this person, so you have magical congruency and a target.
2. Imagine that person's image or the person a way away from you, as though they were the target of the archer on this occasion. Place this image in your line of sight if your head is straight and make the image steady, so you can look away, look back and it's still there.
3. Stand up straight and take a deep breath. Look down on the ground, relax yourself and make sure your pathways are clear and you are getting excited about this coming experience. Note any stress or nervousness and TAKE THAT OUT before you proceed.

1 If in doubt, quickly consult with the person's higher self if it's ok for you to do this. Higher self says no, try someone else.

4. Now and with your eyes still on the ground, think/feel/imagine/evoke the energy of the rising sun. Feel it in your body, feel it running through your body and building up powerfully.
5. Let it build up more and more as you slowly and in time with the rising energy raise your eyes towards the target. Breathe deeply, stay relaxed and enjoy that building sensation of the sunrise energy tingling in your body.
6. Now lock onto the target, take a deep breath in and on the out breath, in a flash, release all that stored up energy towards the target.
7. "Something" will have happened to that energy, to you, and to the target. If it was good enough for a real magic event, you will have seen/felt/heard/experienced something extraordinary, good enough to take your breath away and leave you tingling and amazed.

Please note that if you are a beginner or not used to working with energy this directly, you can expect that your experience of this energy charging and releasing of energy becomes MUCH, MUCH more powerful and profound as you grow in your abilities.

However, you can already use that experience you just had with the sunshine blessing to guide you in the right direction – what you are looking for when you do magic, namely these POWERFUL experiences that will leave you with not a shadow of a doubt that you just did something pretty amazing.

With these magic events, so many questions that people are always asking about spells, potions and rituals DISAPPEAR for good.

People ask, "How will I know that it worked?"

When you've created and experienced a real magic event, even for the first time in practice, you KNOW.

You do not have to ask, "Do I have to do the spell more than once? How many times? How often before I can see the results?"

All of that becomes immaterial – you only do a spell ONCE, it is an EVENT, and the only reason to ever repeat a spell is if you FAILED TO CREATE AN EVENT that you could feel, hear, see, and experience as absolute reality.

You also don't need to worry about the usual advice that you shouldn't look over your shoulder, or keep prodding at the outcomes to "see if anything has happened yet".

With the magic event having occurred, you don't need to second guess yourself or worry – the magic event itself takes care of all of that.

And here is the most important learning about the magic events.

Every magic event changes the magician.

Every time a magic event is created, it literally and in the absolute sense of the word, EMPOWERS THE MAGICIAN.

Every real magic event makes you more powerful.

So it's worth practising this simple base pattern of raising and discharging energy forms to create a change upon a target simply for that fact.

A final note: In the past, people who HAD NOT CLEARED THEIR PATHWAYS FOR MAGIC tried to evoke these change events – and tried to run energy through blocked and dislocated channels. These people ended up HURTING THEMSELVES really badly, and they got sick, and mad, and their magic went crazy as well.

It is possible that the hugely convoluted systems of magic that often seem designed to PREVENT the practitioner from really developing their magical powers, rather than aid themselves in any meaningful way, has arisen in order to protect people from this happening.

If you keep your paths clear, you will be able to not just survive channelling massive amounts of energy but it will in fact serve to enlighten you – further, and further.

Feeling The Magic

To become a really top class practitioner of magic you have to understand that magic is a full body experience, not just a mental game to play.

Before we have any other indication of something working or not working, or going in the right direction or the wrong direction, or if something is true or false, useful or not useful, we need to feel this in our bodies.

In the past, people often got confused between emotions of fear, sadness and stress and the actual feeling that we have when we are interacting with something that is magical in nature.

We have talked about the magic events which are like uncompromising experiences, lightning strikes that rush through your whole body; but on a much lower level, our feelings are the guide to magical existences and experiences first of all – if they are running cleanly.

Once we take out the noise from reversals and negative emotions, "voices" that talk of doom and gloom and the static of jumping mental imagery and adrenaline overdoses in our systems, we FEEL DIFFERENTLY.

This means not just "feeling better" in the general sense of that phrase, but to actively go out and to feel something deliberately, just as you would reach out and feel the rough surface of old stone with your fingertips.

We are used to firstly having all that static in our

feeling systems which really does make them not work properly, and secondly we are not used to using our feeling systems in such a way that they give us clear guidance about occurrences in our environment.

Yet it is our systems of feelings (not emotions!) that guide us through many of the decisions and choices we make when we create a program for change, such as a magic spell, a ritual, or a charm.

Together with clearing the pathways first, we can then set out on a course of learning how to feel for what is right, and what is wrong; and these are very clear cut feelings once you take the noise out of the equation.

Here is a simple exercise for you to try in your own time.

Making An Art Solutions Energy Device Exercise

Say to yourself, say in your mind that you want to create a small drawing that will bring more joy into the room where it is displayed.

Take a pencil and simply let your hand draw a line that loops around on the page, any way it wants to, like this:

Now, take some colours, and keeping in mind that this is an energy magic device you are creating that will bring joy into the room where it displayed, FEEL for the right colour for each segment that is created where the lines have crossed.

What you will notice is that some part of you KNOWS what the right colour is, and that this is a very definite feeling that guides you so you actually can't get it wrong.

Until you have tried this exercise for yourself, you will have to take my word for it that when you get the wrong colour, you get a wrongful feeling, a sense of "No, that's not right!"

When you get the exact right colour, you experience a small rush of energy and excitement – we call this the "click!" when your choice and the magic outcome have clicked together, and you have the right ingredient.

Continue with this exercise until the painting is completed and you have had a full personal experience with knowing something that you cannot "ordinarily know" and being guided exclusively by feelings towards the right choice, in this case of the colours.

Repeat this exercise often and with many different choices so that you can learn more about how you feel for the right thing, and how you experience the "click!" when you get it right.

You can do this, for example, to choose the colours of candles for a particular spell.

Red? Oh no! White? Hmm ... Blue? Yaiks! Green? Hmmm ... Yellow? CLICK! That's the one.

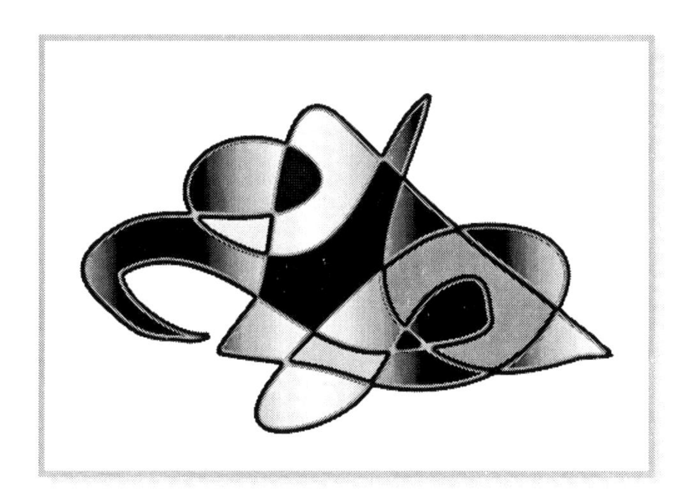

Continue until the symbol painting is finished – congratulations, you have not only created a totally unique, highly personal and fully functional real energy magic generator that will draw energies through it for as long as it exists, but also you have learned a truly powerful new magic skill – you have started to FEEL the magic.

Practice Feeling The Magic

You can and really should practice this core skill of feeling the magic every day and with lots of different things so you get really good at it.

You can practice by letting your feelings choose which kind of charm or jewellery you will be wearing that is right for this day; to choose the correct aromatherapy oil from a selection if you have some handy; you can do this with a choice of fruit from a fruit bowl, drinks from your fridge, which cup to use, which folder to open.

The principle is always the same. Ask the question: Which is the right one for me, right now?

Then FEEL for the answer and listen with your fingertips, with your whole body as you go along the line of comparisons and choices and ask for each one?

This one? That one? That one?

Continue until you FEEL that CLICK! As the right choice makes itself known to you.

Use this for practice to choose movies you watch from a cinema listing; TV programs which you don't know what they might be about; books in a book shop; foods you buy in a supermarket; clothes you buy from a shop and all and any opportunity where choices present themselves to you, and you have to make a decision.

Feeling for the energy components and the magical

components of all these things we have in our environments is perfect practice and also, a great safety device. With a little practice you will be able to tell when people aren't good for you, even though they are smiling and "seem so nice" on the surface; it can warn you that the "lovely soup" you are about to eat will give you food poisoning, and it can tell you which exit is the one that will save your life when the house is on fire.

- **You will be able to rely on your feelings as a PROPER FEEDBACK DEVICE that is just as good as your eyes and ears and adds so much information, and enormous amounts of certainty to your decisions.**

This internal feedback device is a kind of magical compass that shows you the way to the right alignments in all your rituals. It allows you also to test other people's rituals for congruency and whether they are good for you at this time or not.

Remember however to be CLEAR of negative emotions before you make these choices as disturbed emotions, stress, pain and so forth will give you wrongful readings and can lead you to the wrong conclusions.

Once you got the hang of "The Click" you will also recover a HUGE amount of trust in your natural intelligence and intuition, and your confidence with all forms of magic will grow, exponentially so.

Attention & Energy Magic

In the worlds of energy, attention is what gets you where you want to, and attention is what gets things done.

Where you place your attention is where your consciousness will travel to, and where you are directing your own energies in order to change reality.

The law of attention is one of the core principles of energy magic.

Attention tends to be attracted by things we like.

The more we like something, the more our attention is attracted by it.

It is important to understand that attention is not just that movement of us going outside ourselves, reaching out to an object and touching it; at the same time as we are making this movement towards that object of attraction, we are opening a portal that CONNECTS US to the object, and at the same time information and energy starts flowing back to us, bringing with it essential knowledge and understanding about that which we have paid attention to.

The more attention we pay from our end, the more profound this energy exchange becomes, and the more energy flows INTO us in return.

This is experienced as a good feeling, it's a rush of fresh new energy and information, we enjoy this, and this motivates us to pay even more attention, to get even more of this delicious energy coming our way.

At some point in this process, we stop talking about paying attention and start talking about being fascinated by this, and then we may even say, "This is so beautiful, so wonderful, this makes me feel so good – I LOVE this!"

And it is at that point that everything changes, all the barriers crumble and the connection becomes as complete as we know it to be possible – and at the same time, the information and energy exchange has become as good as it can get.

Here is that moment where real magical learning and wisdom is happening – it is then that we truly understand the nature of ... (the bear spirit, the aspen tree, the crystal, the moon, the lord of the rivers, my guardian angel, that person, etc.).

It is really important to understand that this magical connection is absolutely a two way street. Just as you now love the bear spirit, the bear spirit loves you in return. It is here that we can ask it to guide us, help us and even act on our behalf in the spirit world to give us a true heart's desire; to be heard and more importantly, heeded.

If you remember your school days, you will find a direct correlation between those subjects and topics that you liked, and how much you learned about them.

Compare this with the subjects you didn't like, and note that you didn't learn very much about those, if anything at all.

More importantly still, which lessons did you look forward to, and which did you find pleasurable? In other words, which inspired you to learn even more about the topic?

You can see how rejection actively stops us from learning, and acceptance, attention, attraction and eventually, love, will make us learn so much more – and have a joyful time while we are learning and discovering new things about that.

When we are working with the symbols, it is clear that the more you love the entire set of symbols, and each one individually, you will get the most pleasure and the best results from your symbol set.

A really important part of that energy exchange is information – and we need the information that comes through the symbols to us to make decisions on every aspect of every spell, ritual or potion we will make.

We need to know what colour, what plant; what time of day, what time of year; which entity is best placed to help us with this; what to do, step by step, and all of that information will stream gladly to you, so fast that it can be like a flash of a vision that contains so much knowledge – and knowledge you can PRACTICALLY USE to do real magic, and to do real magic well.

If you see the symbols in front of you right now, you would find that one or another will attract your attention.

The reason our attention becomes attracted is that we think there's something good for us there, something important that will help us if we know about it.

This works both for guiding us to the tastiest, ripest berries or some fresh sparkling water in the distance, as well as warning us that there is a potential danger that should be avoided.

Either way, whatever we become attracted to IS IMPORTANT.

Understanding Magic Failure

In energy magic, there is nothing you can't do, there is nothing you can't reach, there is nothing you can't touch, and there's nothing you can't change. And if you can't change "it" you can change your attitude towards "it" and then it becomes a resource rather than something that hurts or hinders you.

In energy magic, we are not trying to move physical objects with our minds or make physical demons materialise in the physical world, and we don't get on physical broomsticks to ride around in the physical rain, get wet and die of pneumonia.

These things are all metaphorical misunderstandings, as happens often in magic as it does in so many other places.

When I talk to young people who might have become interested in magic because they saw Harry Potter and tell them this, they become very upset and say, "What? Do you mean I don't get to fly on real broomstick for real?"

I shrug my shoulders and say, "No, you can't. At least not as it stands at the moment, at this phase of our development, and with the local conventions we've got going on here, there is nobody on this planet, and there has NEVER been anyone on this planet, who can get on a broomstick and fly up into the air."

So the youngsters are bitterly disappointed and depressed, and I say, "Why is this depressing you?

"Imagine for a moment that you were a real witch, and you had a husband, and you were suspecting the husband was having an affair with his secretary at work.

"So you get on your broomstick and it happens to be a freezing November night and it's raining, hard.

"You get yourself drenched to the bone as you fly to his office building in the city, and the winds are particularly nasty as well, buffeting you as you're clinging to your broomstick with your cold, wet, clammy, shaking fingers.

"And so you finally get there, and you hover outside the window in the storm, watching your husband do his thing with the secretary on the desk in the 30th floor office, and you're freezing your backside off – what is the benefit of that?

"Would you not much rather stay somewhere nice and cosy, safe and warm and instantly travel in your astral body to this office and stand there, invisible to all, to see what goes on?

"Which one is more elegant? Which one is more useful? Which one is more elegant? And most of all; which approach has more scope?

"If you were trying to fly to the moon on your broomstick – and don't get me started about the problems of re-entering the atmosphere on the way back! - you'd be freezing to death already by the time you get to 50,000 feet. There's no oxygen up there for your physical body. It's a nightmare, and it doesn't work. Are you going to get on your broomstick in a space suit?

"Staying safe at home and astral travelling to wherever you want to go is far more elegant, logical, safe and makes a whole lot more sense.

"I can't see how anyone could POSSIBLY be disappointed that they can't balance on a slippery broomstick!"

Energy magic is about working with energetic realities, not about hacking pieces of rock out of a mountain side "with your mind".

Don't be disappointed by this.

Instead, be delighted.

- **EVERYTHING has an energetic component to it and that means ANYTHING is touchable by real energy magic.**

As the energy levels and dimensions are such an undiscovered country to humanity, there is ENORMOUS room for exploration and for leverage there, and you can do things that simply can't be done in any other way with energy magic – and that is right, and proper.

We have tremendous leverage over all and any energetic system and **people forget this.**

We call this phenomenon "magic failure".

Magic failure is when the Universe collapses and becomes "only hard" through stress, pain and fear and a person thinks or says, "I'm all alone." - "There is nothing I can do." - "It's too hard." - "It's all over." - "This is my only option." - "Nobody loves me." - "This will never work." - "I don't have a choice." - "It can't be done." - "There is no hope."

You can literally ONLY think like that, feel like that, when you have lost contact with the greater reality of the real true living Universe – these thoughts, ideas and emotions denote not any kind of truth, but simply that YOU ARE IN MAGIC FAILURE.

The magic symbol reminds us that you are not alone, that there **is** something (many things!) you can do, that it's not too hard, that there are multiple options, always, that you are loved and that you do belong to the greater scheme of things, and that "it" can be done – and there are many ways to do it, right now.

The Magic symbol is the portal to the magical domains of energy where we are truly free to fly, and to move about as we please; to experiment, to work and pray, to live and learn at our own leisure, each one of us.

Magic failure is one of those things that happens to everyone, even the greatest magician can experience moments of magic failure if they are put under too much stress, they become too unstable and then lose contact with the fine, light filled energy dimensions that empower us so much.

The most important thing is to get out of magic failure as soon as possible, and by using the Magic symbol in our environments to remind us of the magic is our safety anchor to get back with the program, get back with the real world from which we got disconnected in a moment of stress and trauma.

The Symbol Pantheon

I am going to offer something interesting that you might find useful.

Instead of the magician directly influencing energetic realities, magic often uses the idea that another will act on their behalf - an entity such as an angel or a demon, a guide, a servitor, a friend, a saint, a deity and so forth.

People who have been doing serious magic and witchcraft for any length of time obviously already have a working pantheon established

Pantheon means "all Gods" and is a "full set of Gods" from a single religion or spiritual approach. For example, the Romans had their pantheon, the Greeks and Celts and Egyptians had theirs, and the Christians used saints to fill that place between the Creative Force of the Universe and which is unknowable in all ways, and the people on the other side with these super power beings. Modern witches often borrow Gods and Goddesses, angels and saints from a wide variety of different pantheons and put them together to form a personal pantheon they find works for them.

It takes a long time to assemble a pantheon; in the Genius Symbols, you have a working pantheon you can use right away and at the same time as you learn to tune towards the energy domains for which each symbol is the portal.

So for example you can pretty much from the start address "the spirit of the animals" (the lord/lady of the animals, the God of the animals) using the animal symbol as the portal.

That is the same for all the symbols; from the Lord of the Dance to the spirit of The Light, and from the Plant God to the Spirit of Time - here you have a simple but immensely powerful pantheon that will work from the word "go!"

In order to make this work, you don't have to believe anything at all or subscribe to any form of religion; and these symbol spirits work perfectly well together with other deities and spirits from established religious pantheons, in fact, you might even find that some of them are the same.

"The Spirit of ..." is the highest level of consciousness in the symbols, very powerful indeed, and if you make good friends with these energy forms, pay attention and effectively allow yourself to fall in love with all of them, you will have a pantheon on your side that you can really work with, and that will empower you enormously.

Try it for yourself.

Contemplate for a moment what it would be like if "The Lord of Time was on my side" or you had the unwavering support of "The Spirit Of Crystal". As to the spirit of all angels, the spirit of the light, that is breath taking in its pure beauty and potential for helping you right here, in this life time, and with your expanding magic.

The Gift

One of the most important and most powerful concepts in energy magic is that of "The Gift".

The Gift is the basis of all ritual offerings humans make to create a relationship and an exchange between them and someone else.

This holds true for giving gifts inside close family relationships; it holds true for giving gifts to others so that they open themselves up for trade and commerce, and good will; and this also exists at yet another level for making offerings to spirits and deities.

What people who don't do magic don't understand is that when you place some grain on the altar of a deity, or a flower in a special place in your garden for the fairies, or even when you give your husband a new tie of a pleasing colour, this is NOT about the material objects.

What is being offered as a The Gift is an energy form; and this is where things become extremely interesting.

When you make offerings and give The Gift to any being, entity, landscape, object, deity, situation even, you can very literally "give of yourself" - create a The Gift that is absolutely uniquely yours, that comes from you and through you, and that makes the perfect offering in every way.

Even with people in the hard, the best gifts are personal

and spontaneous, unique and surprising, and that is the same with the energy forms we give when we give The Gift.

Once again, consciously we cannot know what the right The Gift for any purpose would be; we have to let this come to us from our energy mind, we have to receive a quick vision that tells us what the perfect The Gift for this moment, this time, this entity would be.

Try it.

If at this moment you would give a The Gift as an offering to your Guardian Angel, what would it be?

Don't think about it; just let it come to you, and DO NOT JUDGE THE GIFT.

It might be something that seems small and insignificant, like a child's toy for example, or a simple household object that springs to mind.

You might think, "Oh no! I can't possibly give a little toy horse made from plastic to my Guardian Angel! That's not good enough! It has to be something much more expensive and grand and enlightened!"

And yet, and in this example, when the small toy plastic horse was given to the Guardian Angel, that angel was as close to being moved to tears by this gift as any angel ever could be and received it with the greatest honour.

Please understand: To be able to give The Gift, without reservation, from the heart and soul, PERSONALLY from you, is one of the most priceless, most precious core skills of an energy magician.

You can change just about any situation, any relationship with anything at all by giving The Gift.

YOU have an infinite amount of The Gifts to come through you and manifest for that entity.

And even with angels, or really, really high up beings, it may just be the case that they are awaiting such gifts from folk like us, and that somehow these help THEM evolve in some way.

To give The Gift, and to give it freely, is immensely empowering and very powerful magic indeed.

My advice is to practice this all the time, giving these energy gifts to everyone you love, everyone you meet, in the hard and on the many different realms of existence, and notice how that makes you feel, how that helps you grow.

Receiving The Gift

It is so that just as you have a The Gift for everything and everyone you will ever meet, they have a The Gift for you.

They might not say to you, "Well, here's my gift, it's a wonderful green energy form that will make you feel happy and well."

They might not say anything at all, but it is incumbent upon you to find out what your "The Gift" is. To embrace it, take it in, allow it to come to you, flow through you and ultimately change you.

Learn to ask yourself, "What is my The Gift here?" when you are interacting with friends, aliens, landscapes, crystals, stars, beings and deities and actively open yourself up to receive this The Gift fully and completely.

To do this takes a level of maturity, trust, understanding and love because you are allowing yourself to be changed by this The Gift - and that is a form of gift in and of itself once more to the giver, that you would trust them and love them enough that you would accept and embrace that gift they have offered you.

THE 23 GENIUS SYMBOLS

Space

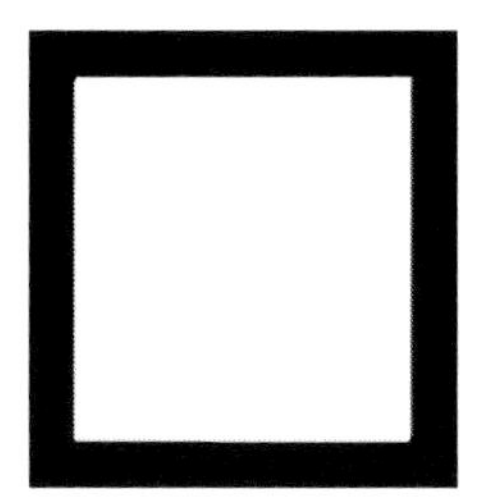

A simple square that denotes all things relating to space, including physical space, mental space, the distance between objects, journeys to travel, north, south, east, west, up and down, and across as well.

This is a multi-dimensional space; space in the widest sense but also in the most practical, down to Earth sense, such as "Do you have enough space?" Enough space to express yourself, enough space to expand your wings, the right space to be working in at this time, and much besides.

There are a lot of mental entrainments about our physical spaces, for example there is a common size to rooms that people are living in and this impacts their idea of their own size, and the size of their energy bodies.

There are many entrainments from the hard such as "long distances" and "it's harder to go up than down" and the idea that you can own space by buying a piece of it which make no sense in the worlds of energy at all.

Here, there are no distances and there is freedom from gravity to mention just two features that make flying to anywhere very easy – if we can let it be that easy, that is.

Thinking of yourself as small and feeble in physical size, in the many dimensions a magician will travel, is also an entrainment that doesn't serve us well at all.

Mastery over space and your relationship to space allows you to find the right size for the right endeavour and gives you a lot of flexibility and leverage over so many systems.

This is a fascinating symbol, very basic, very powerful and often a key to make important changes on many levels; this is also the symbol we use for all forms of astral travel in energy magic.

Time

Time is one of those things that nobody really understands correctly or how to use it correctly. Conversely, time is one of those symbols that once you start connecting with the spirit of it, it will give you a lot more understanding of many things. For example, many activities and experiences in our societies are broken up into bits and pieces, but time reconnects them all, makes something that was broken, whole again.

Time connects a person's life, and it connects up a person's day as well, even when the activities that happened during that day seemed so different.

Also, one of the most difficult things in magic for beginners is to locate the time of something correctly.

For example, you may have a premonition of an airplane crashing and it is clear in every detail - but WHEN is this going to happen? In an hour?

Tomorrow? Next week? Has it already happened? Without the time co-ordinates, the information is next to useless. Likewise, if you are making a success spell for someone else, how do you know where to position this correctly in time? Not too quick, not too far away, so that it fits in with that person's time of life?

There are whole libraries of writings on how to find the right time for a spell and how important it is for luck, synchronicity and all sorts of things to be not only in the right place, but to be there at the right time.

Working with the time symbol (and making friends with the spirit of time!) greatly improves our understanding of time itself, and with that, improves our accuracy and our ability to place intentions at the right time - to do things in the right order and sequence and with the best support that time has to offer.

Having this growing understanding about how time works also solves that old magic riddle of the ages and improves your ability to know just WHEN something will come to pass, to read the time correctly in a vision and to know that you need to do something on Tuesday at 5 o'clock, rather than at any other time.

Time is well worth spending some time on understanding better because time is one of the core aspects that make our Universe work the way it does, and with a good understanding of time, magic becomes much more accurate in every way.

Weather

The weather is a really important aspect of our natural world. It determines if anything can grow, it shapes the landscape, creates the environment, decides if anyone can live there at all, and if so, how difficult that is going to be.

The weather sets the tone and scene for all the activities that plants, animals and people are performing as the year goes by.

The weather is alive and it has a purpose; it has a destiny, a future and a past, it owns the space where it happens and it is a most fascinating thing indeed.

Most witches are deeply connected to and fascinated by the weather; and that is on the level of the weather happening outside our doors amazingly, and majestically, all the time.

But that is just one level of weather. There is also the "universal weather" or what is called astrology; influences that are travelling through the Universe and that affect everyone profoundly, even though they might never know where any of this has come from.

And when we pull that symbol right down and back to ourselves, the weather is about our emotions, our changing states in our energy system.

When I use the term "emotions" I don't just mean Disney movie type emotions - you cry, you laugh, you cry again.

Our internal weather can have furious lightning storms and lightning strikes of enlightenment; powerful movements, rivers of information flowing through us, blue skies and rich waters.

So you can see that the weather symbol is very powerful and has everything to do with experience in the real world, and how we relate to the changes in our environment, how we respond, and most importantly in magic, how we USE this weather to help us achieve what we want.

Think of it in terms of hanging your washing out to dry when it is sunny (but not when it is raining!) and bringing out a dry pot plant to revive in the rain. When we understand the weather on all these levels, and work with it successfully, more than half of magic is already done for us without expending any energy on our behalf - just like using the wind to sail across the oceans, or thermal updrafts that are the wind beneath our wings.

The Land

The land is the material structure that underlies everything. Without a planet, there can be no primordial soup in which life might be happening.

This symbol stands for the land as in "the lay of land" - the mountains, the valleys, the deep sea beds, the landscape as it is unfolding and developing. At the energy levels, the land draws our attention to the energetic structures of the land, environmental energy, leylines, earth rivers and so forth.

As we go outward, the land stands for the structures that are the planets and suns and what holds them in place, and it stands for the real supporting structures that hold the Universe together. This is not just material or energetic but also about the structure of principles, laws of nature.

If we take the land to the personal level, we have the landscape of our physical bodies, the structures that hold our bodies together and the structures of the energy system.

Please note that although we are talking about structures here and principles, the land also evolves in its own time; so it is not and never rigid, as nothing in the true Universe would be, but it unfolds and it is alive.

The Crystal

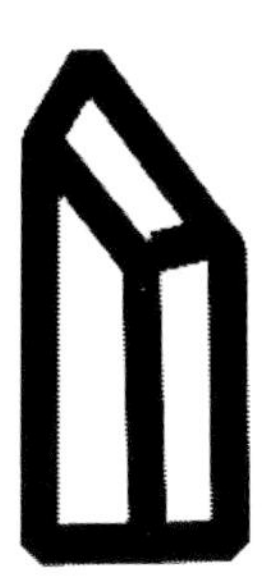

The Crystal stands for real crystals, as representatives of the crystal kingdom which are fantastic messengers, so rich with energy and information about many things, so beautiful to behold, and fantastic to work with in magic.

At another level, the Crystal symbol also stands for clarity and logic. We have already talked about the "medieval crazy ideas" born out of terror, pain and confusion, and what was clearly missing there was any kind of real clarity, any real logic.

Logic has been given a bad name over the centuries and people think that it has no emotion in it, no compassion, no love, but there is nothing more logical than love, and if it is done right, there is nothing more loving than logic.

The Universe is deeply logical; it functions in beauty and in logic. True logic is breathtaking in its beauty also, in its clarity and it does have emotion that comes with it - transcendental joy, ecstasy of the highest order, and such unconditional love, it takes your breath away.

For people who have misunderstood logic to be cold and heartless number crunching and have rejected it because of that, it can be a fantastic revelation to see logic come alive and that it is as beautiful as a multi-faceted crystal which carries rainbows inside itself.

The Plant

This symbol stands for the entire plant kingdom, it is the basis for life and it holds life now.

The plant kingdom has so much power of pure life and healing, it is extraordinary in every way.

People sometimes forget that there is more to the green life than monocultures of rice or wheat, and the odd apple tree or two. The plant kingdom encompasses an extraordinary array of different forms of existence, different frequencies and different vibrations, and all so called higher forms of life are already pre-supposed here, exist here as an idea, a potential.

The most important thing about the plant kingdom however is the life force energy of which it is the ambassador. It takes the energy from the sun and makes it so that we can process it, take it into ourselves, and so the plant kingdom structurally connects us to the stars in the sky, and the Universe at large.

To have a good relationship with the spirit of the plant kingdom is a gift of priceless proportions because there is a level of existence at which we are members of this kingdom, as well as being its descendant and child.

The Animal

After the plants on planet Earth, there came the animals, and these could walk around and think in a different way; they could also act in a different way.

The animals were a new order of life and eventually we human beings arose from there; but it is worth noting that we still share 98% of our genetic heritage with the chimpanzees.

We are much closer to the animal kingdom than most of us would like to believe; and when we talk about animals, we do not mean that medieval nonsense of "dirty filthy animals.

We are talking about basic survival, to be able to see and hear; to move away from danger and towards good things and delicious things; to want to mate and produce offspring, to have instincts and a natural understanding of how to live in this world that evolved together with us, hand in hand.

Through the animal ancestry, we are directly linked into the ancestry of life on this planet.

The Animal symbol also stands for any representative of the animal kingdom, real animals alive or in the spirit world; animal spirits, totems, familiars and guardians.

The Human Being

The "people" symbol is the one that most people will have the most problems with, as all our injuries, physical, emotional and spiritual derive to 99% from other people - of course.

It is especially important to "clear the paths" as relate to this symbol, because having a good foundation in a loving relationship with your own species is a bit of a pre-requisite to be able to act as a human being, and activate human magic correctly.

A single human being as a "human totality" consists of a fabulous array of levels and layers that are all in flow and should all be evolving; we speak of mind, body and spirit but once in a while it serves well to sit down and really get in touch with what that really means.

I do not believe that we can either understand magic or practice magic correctly (or even at all) until and unless we have explored what a human being is in general, and what that means for each one of us as individuals.

Something that is worth bearing in mind is that a single human being is not either male or female, and that nearly everything we are taught about male and female energies and how that leads to men being better than women, or men doing the hunting and women doing the housework (or cave work, if you will!), and that men do esoteric "high" magic and women do "low" kitchen magic is all nothing but purest bullshit.

There is every merit in really going for clearing those ideas and blockages to what REAL HUMAN MAGIC can be like from your systems, and that includes anger and rage women have inherited from medieval witches traditions just as much as it includes the terror that men have inherited from medieval manifestations of mad emotions.

Disconnecting yourself from these swirling powerfields of the ages and claiming your right to be a human being first of all, and then to EXPLORE WHAT THAT MEANS for yourself is the only safe and loving way to proceed.

Making contact with the true spirit of the human being, understanding what that is, and having a profound love based relationship with that is the key to working magic at all, and most certainly, on working magic that includes human beings and their acts in any way along the line. This symbol represents a delicious challenge to anyone who really wants to know and use their magic, and in many ways is the master key to magic as a whole.

The House

Unlike a crystal, time or an animal, a house is something that is made by people. People make houses for shelter and for protection, and to confine and separate themselves from the Universe around them.

I would like to make the note that the house has been said to be a metaphor for the human body, as in "my body is a temple". This is a very damaging and erroneous metaphor because the body belongs to the Creative Order, is made by the Creative Order, and not by people. In this context, we can say that the house would be the construct idea made by the conscious mind as to what the body is and it has nothing to do with actual reality itself.

As the house is a construct, built by human beings for their own purposes and with their own hands, this symbol represents the works of men in a very global sense, the practical sphere of influence and also that mindspace that is sometimes called "the box" - as in,

"You need to learn to think outside the box".

On another level, the house denotes practically where you live and your physical surroundings that you have constructed and moved into.

Houses can be powerful protectors and allies, as well as become prisons of our own making across the levels and layers so this symbol is very much about reality creation in the hard by human beings, how we do that, why we do that, and to pay attention to this and how it can be used, and improved.

The Aspect

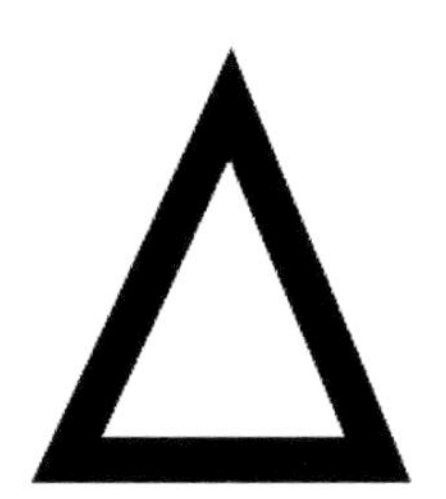

The Aspect is a single facet of a large diamond which has many facets; and it tells us that if we want to see the whole picture, understand the entirety of any thing, entity or situation, we need to keep fluent, keep moving, and take up many different points of view, all of which will reveal further aspects of the whole to us.

This includes the aspects of a person, for example; someone might have aspects that are very good and honourable, and other aspects that are angry and violent. They "are" neither one nor the other, but a greater totality that embraces all the aspects and brings them together in something that is far more than just the sum of its parts (or aspects).

All things have many aspects; every situation has different aspects too, and this symbol asks us to keep fluent, not get stuck on a single point of view for any length of time, and to consider other aspects on the same situation, the same person, the same required outcome.

Magic

The symbol for magic is the spiral.

When I was first given this symbol, I saw a galaxy; and I understood that magic is not just an invisible manifestation but that it is integral and a part of the greater Universe that contains the invisible as well as the visible, altogether.

Magic brings us back to the material universe as well, so when that happens then the entire world becomes our home.

The magic symbol reminds us that we are not powerless in the Universe; that we have the power of action both in the physical as well as the energetic levels and layers of the world in which we live.

The Dance

The Dance symbol is the connection and the give and take, the interdependence in the flow of energy and information.

People are very given to chopping up reality into "one thing, or another".

This is red, this is blue; this is hard, this is soft; this is up, this is down; this is east and that is west.

The truth is that reality doesn't work like that, it isn't made up of separate bits but there is always a dance that is happening between everything, and everything is dancing.

For all situations, it takes more than just "two to tango".

Everything is connected in the dance. When you find yourself in trouble, or you don't know what to do, to step into the dance is the first (dance) step to take part again, and once you are inside of the dance, you might then be able to lead that dance in a new direction.

This is a very powerful and important symbol and one that once you really understand it can give you tremendous leverage, but also wonder, and joy that is the heart of the dance.

The Alien

We people live here on planet Earth and we think that we've seen it all, and we know it all, but the fact is that we don't.

One of the things I find particularly fascinating is that the only reason we think of metal as cold, strong and hard is because of the local conventions that exist here on Planet Earth.

The same metal, on another planet, might be a warm liquid that flows in rivers, or it might be a gas that forms clouds in the sky, or it may be a frozen, fragile crystal instead.

Looking at your situations through the eyes of an alien once in a while, and to remember that what we know and what we are used to here is not the whole story is a powerful and empowering experience that can give us completely new solutions to old, "stuck, cold, hard" problems that have dodged people since time began.

This symbol also denotes aspects of ourselves that are

alien in origin and alien in nature; and of course quite practically refers to real aliens, alien spirits and alien souls.

There is a tremendous amount of information and excitement in this symbol, as it is the doorway to alien domains across the levels and the layers.

The Spirit

This symbol asks us to leave the physical world and all its concerns behind for the time being and concentrate on the spirit world.

Often, this symbol refers to the spirits of dead people - ancestors, family members, friends and others that are linked or important in the context and who have information or may take action to bring about a desired outcome.

This symbol can also refer to special companion animals who were once alive and now are in the spirit world but who have retained their connection to a person.

On a more global level, this symbol also encompasses "the spirit of a thing" - the spirit of a landscape, of a business, of an idea, the resonance of that thing/object/situation at the spirit level.

The Artefact

The artefact is a man made object with magical powers. An artefact does not necessarily have to have been shaped into a recognisable form by the hand of man, such as a chalice or a book or a tool of some kind; people can also create artefacts by changing the energetic reality of a material object so it becomes a resonant magical object even if it looks just like a rock or a pebble to the uninitiated.

Of course, when you make your set of Genius Symbols, every one of those markers has become an artefact, even if it was only a piece of glass or stone or wood when it started out.

Artefacts are always active portals to their own reality.

When you go into a person's house, you will see innumerable objects there, but only some of those are artefacts, objects that "tell a story".

The world of artefacts is very interesting, and includes all charms, amulets, magical tools and magical works of art.

The making of magical objects that then continue to act in a magical and active fashion on the world is one of the first and core skills of magical workings; and so for magicians especially, the artefact symbol is a power symbol and extremely important.

The Star

This symbol stands for The Light.

The light is arguably the most powerful force in the Universe; some think of it as being inseparable from God itself, the highest, the all-there-is.

Our star is the sun, and on a level, the sun is the metaphor for the soul, and the sunrise is the metaphor for the awakening of the human soul, of the beginning of a person's true immortality.

The Light is all around us, and we speak of becoming enlightened, of being delighted, and I often talk of being "light" (as opposed to heavy) in our dealings with magic and the spirit world is of the essence to get magic right, and to be able to reach and touch the true heart of magic itself.

On a practical level, "shedding more light" onto any situation will allow you to "see things in a new light" and when you add The Light to any work of magic, be it a little spell for every day or a great and beautiful tapestry you are weaving over decades, it takes a threshold shift into something more profound and beautiful in every way.

Light sparkles, it is beautiful, it makes beauty happen, so let this light lift you, raise your spirits and delight you - it belongs to you by right of birth.

The Fountain

The Fountain denotes genesis, and creativity.

On the grand cosmic level, this is the force that gave birth to the entire Universe, all the stars, all the planets, all the life.

As you are bringing this down to the levels of people and their magic, this creativity becomes expressed in our ideas and what we make with our hands as we too become "mini-creators".

It is in the act of creativity that we reconnect with the force that created everything and it is rightfully held to be one of the holiest activities.

It is important to not get creativity mixed up with creating huge works of art that take decades of skilled labour to perfect; creativity is as basic as drawing a symbol in the soft sand on a beach, or making a pendant from a stone and a piece of string that holds meaning for you.

Creativity becomes expressed in magic, and it is at the

centre of magic, as a person creates spells and rituals to make changes according to their will, their purpose.

There is also then the aspect of The Fountain that relates to matters of conception, birth, rebirth and creation in that sense of life re-creating itself through itself, and evolution.

The Gift

The Gift is another one of the core skills of magic, and we discuss the Gift in that sense in another part of this book.

In the sense of The Gift as a symbol in the symbol sphere, the Gift denotes a form of energy that is not an exchange, but indeed A GIFT.

That means you can't buy it, you can't do anything to deserve it, all you can do is to ask for gifts, and receive them if they come your way with open arms.

In that sense a gift is a miracle; and there is the aspect of the gift being a surprise, being unexpected and out of the ordinary.

We have the power to bestow The Gift as well as we have the power to receive these gifts; and we must understand that just as a gift that comes to us is unconditional, so is a gift when we give it.

If you give something to receive something in return,

that's not a gift, it's a trade and there is nothing wrong with that at all, you just need to know the difference.

The Trade

A trade is an exchange, a system that relies on give and take. Whereas a gift is a one way energy discharge, a trade is to give and receive.

We spoke about how we pay attention and thus we open a channel where we receive information and energy in return; this is a classic example of a trade based system.

At the basic human level, the trade is about the way we take in nutrition, water, air and so forth and give back to the environment in equal measure.

Following from that, all matters of human commerce are also in the domain of the Trade symbol - buying and selling, exchange of goods, business dealings and so forth.

There is a "spirit of The Trade" that is little understood amongst people who do business in a negative and selfish way, or who are used to it being that way because that's all they know.

The real spirit of The Trade is a fabulous and very, very powerful thing that enriches all those who take part in the trade (and that may be many, many more than just two parties giving and taking) in the very process of engaging in this trade, and regardless of what goodies may be the eventual outcome of the trade having taken place.

Trade also refers to communication and the flow of communication so if, for example, you are having problems "communicating with the angels" then connecting with the spirit of fair trade (ie, beautiful trade) is going to help with that.

The Angel

The Angel symbol stands for all higher powers, not just angels but also including angels.

When I use the term "higher" powers, I do not mean that they are somehow better than us, but simply that they live in domains of higher frequencies and so they don't manifest like people would, rocks, or plants, but in a different way.

This symbol may include ascended masters, ascended prophets, deities and other beings of intelligence that may be contacted by us at this time and who have an active interest in what we are doing.

There are many worlds of divergent and active intelligences behind this simple symbol, and it also includes those aspects of a living human being which are in contact with those many worlds; sometimes called "the higher self".

There is a tremendous amount of fascinating energy

forms, information and very proactive help and assistance to be found in these domains, so this symbol is extremely important in the overall scheme of things.

The Friend

A Friend is a spirit guide, an advisor that lives at a level which lies in between the angel dimensions and where we humans normally choose to put our attention.

I cannot tell you definitively exactly who or what friends are, but I can tell you that there are many entities out there who are ready and willing to form a close, PERSONAL relationship with you and help guide your way in the many worlds, and all those many different dimensions.

I think it is possible that friends were once very corporeal, like we are still ourselves, and that they represent an after death evolved form of beings such like ourselves.

This is quite different from angels or deities which were never human in the first place and so often simply lack an understanding of the problems we experience in our embodied states.

The friends know about the challenges and the excitement we people have about the many worlds, and they can help us immeasurably if only we let them do just that.

How much support each individual magician is willing to receive and draw upon from friends is entirely up to them; but I would make the note that most people don't use the friends they could have or even the ones they have already found to anywhere near their full potential.

Friends are 100% on your side; they help you unconditionally and your evolution is their highest priority.

So it is also a function of this symbol that we humans can too act as "The Friend" to another human being if we choose to do so - to help someone unconditionally on THEIR path, and this service being your first and most important reward, not gratitude or payments of any other kind.

DragonWings

The spirit rising, astral travelling, the human spirit soaring high in flight resembles that of a dragon, or a bird, or an angel - it is an energy form with wings and it is made entirely of light.

The amazing thing about people is that they can assume this shape and travel where they will even before they are dead; many do in dreams or by accident, but it is a structural capability of all humans to let their spirit rise up, quite practically, and see the whole world in a different way altogether and from a different perspective too.

The DragonWings symbol is therefore an invitation to step up and through and let your spirit fly to places in space and time where it may have experiences, find learnings, answers, and ACT in a way that our human physical body never could.

In order to activate the spirit body it is incumbent upon us to let go of ideas of the physical body we are so used to, with the two eyes and arms and the legs, and fully inhabit that other body, the one that was made for travelling in those other dimensions.

Across the ages, people have had terrible problems with entering into those other dimensions and dragging their human shape and all their preconceptions with them where it didn't belong; in your astral shape, these other planes are natural to you and you can navigate there in comparative safety, and having all the right systems, tools and resources to be able to survive there, and to thrive there.

"Seeing a situation through the eyes of your dragon" (or your spirit self, or your energy angel, if you will) changes many things and can tell you just about all you need to know about the magical and other dimensional properties and influences on any given person, object or situation.

Star Dust

This symbol opens the gate to that dimension where all things are pure potential, and that level where all things are star dust, absolute.

The Christians have the dour saying of "Ashes to ashes, dust to dust" but as usual, that's that negative, Dark Ages take on the WONDERFUL and light filled understanding that all things come from sparkling pure potential, and will return to sparkling pure potential in the end.

We are made of star dust, and that's true, and wonderful.

We often talk about using this symbol to "sprinkle a little fairy dust" on any given person, object or situation; and by doing so, revealing the ENORMOUS potential that exists in everything at the most profound and basic level.

All Symbols

So these are the 23 symbols:

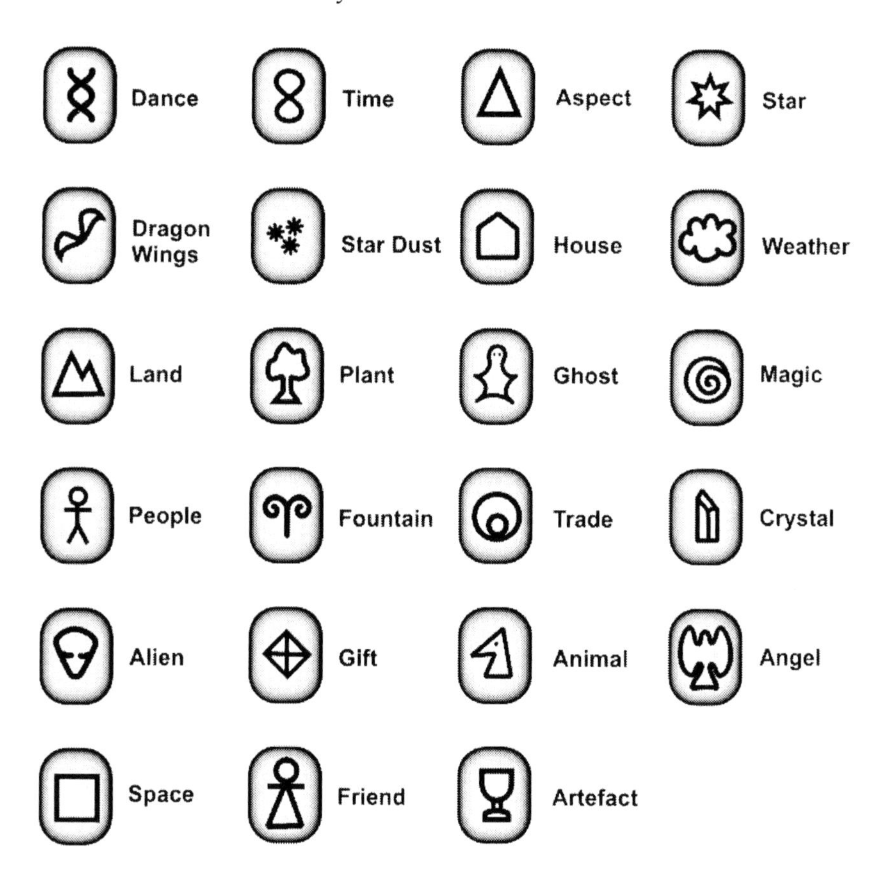

I would recommend that you take your time, make your first symbol set, and get to know these portals and the energy forms that lie behind them.

Here are the instructions.

Your First Symbol Set

We have already mentioned the principle that the more attracted you are to something and the more attention you pay to it in turn, the more you love something, the deeper and more profound your connection to this becomes.

The more you love something, the more information and energy will stream from it towards you, through you, and the better it feels, the more exciting and the more rewarding the entire relationship becomes.

In this spirit, think about making your first symbol set in such a way that you will find it attractive, and that it will be attracting you and make it easy for you to pay that attention that will bring the great rewards.

- **In practice, this means to start with base templates of something you really love and treasure.**

Some people just love wood, and if you are one of those, make your symbol set from wood. Some people love crystal, so make your symbol set from crystal. Some people love pebbles, some love glass, some love metal most of all; it is individual and entirely up to you what you want to choose for your own first deck.

But do be sure that you use your fascination and attraction to give that baseline of connection to your own first symbol set.

There is an important note here that this is in fact, your FIRST symbol set. You will make many more, different ones for different occasions; and of course you will be using the symbols themselves in many different ways, and on many different objects and situations.

So be light and joyous in your heart before you start; find templates that are really pleasing and attractive to you, and that is more than 50% of the job done, right here at the start.

I am going to take you through a very simple and basic symbol sphere activation process, a ritual if you will, that you can use right away with your first symbol set.

For your next set, or perhaps the one after that, you will make your own ritual, one that you are guided to making using the methods and devices we will talk about in a moment and that will then represent a further threshold shift into your next level of mastery.

For now, here is the First Symbol Set Activation Ritual.

First Symbol Set Activation Ritual

1. Assemble your templates - remember to choose something very attractive to you, this is of the essence.

2. Create a special protected time and place where you will dedicate the set and wake it up so it becomes active and ready to use. You will need about an hour of truly undisturbed time in a positive and supporting environment.

3. Follow this step by step for every one of the symbols.

    - Pick a blank template and hold it to your heart.
    - Have a symbol come to you and say with your voice AND think with your mind in chorus at the same time, "I dedicate you to (name the symbol)."
    - As best you can at this time, let the energy flow from the Universe (where these energy forms live) into you, through you, through your heart and hands and into the symbol template.
    - You can feel when it is complete, and the symbol template has been "filled" with this energy, aligned to this energy form like iron filings align

  themselves to a magnet, and has become a portal for that energy form.
- Now draw the symbol onto the template as best you can which seals the change.
- Kiss the symbol (kiss of life) and welcome it with love and place it into your developing symbol sphere.

Continue until all 23 symbols have been placed and the symbol sphere is complete.

4. Now sit back in your mind and contemplate the symbol sphere as a whole, as a single entity, a magical machine or a magical being in its own right, something that is here to help you, to support you and to be unquestioningly on your side.

   Allow the symbol sphere to form a single sphere of energy that rises up and allow this energy to flow into you, through and out as you give it your best attention, admiration and love with your heart and soul in return.

5. To conclude, hold out your hands in a receiving as well as a blessing gesture over the symbols and say,

   "I welcome you into my world, so that you may serve my highest path, in light and love.

   "This is my will."

6. Bow and now you should leave the sphere for 24

hours to settle; the next day, you can start to use this magic entity for making your own magic, for real.

Some practical notes:

It is perfectly ok to look up the symbols in the book as you go through the dedication process, one at a time.

Don't worry about not being able to draw, paint or apply the symbols absolutely perfectly. As long as the symbol is recognisable, it will work just fine.

Remember the "clearing the paths" exercise if you should find a symbol not being as lovable as any of the others, or if you discover blocks or confusions along the way in the dedication ceremony.

With this first dedication, just do the best you can. Your best is more than good enough for the powers that be! They will be very impressed - as will all your future selves! - how well you did under the circumstances, so be light of heart, and know that this is a first step to get you started and that's all it is.

Now your symbol "magic machine" is ready for use, and we can start to talk about how to make some fabulous magic, spells, potions, charms, and even complex rituals with the help of our new friendly symbols.

TRAVEL IN THE MAGIC REALMS

The first thing for any magician, any witch, any person who wants to learn magic is to be able to travel in the magic realms and bring back information, energy forms, resources and to acquire help and support in all your magic endeavours.

A single human being, no matter how clever, simply cannot learn to do magic without access to these realms, or without such personalised support systems.

There are literally infinite dimensions, realms and planes of existence; in the past, this has confused the living daylights and all sanity out of people who were helplessly being catapulted by random sufferings and substance abuses here, there and everywhere and couldn't make any sense of any of it.

To avoid their sad fate and start a proper exploration of the magic realms and what we can do with them, I have devised the concept of the Sanctuary realms, and this is where we will travel for now to get our help, support and information.

We have to rely on our energy mind and its inherent connections with the greater Universe to take us to the right places in time and space to meet the right entities, get the right information we require, and get the jobs done we want to get done.

This is made easy by the use of the symbols; and the first and most important job of the symbols is to take us to those rightful places in time and space in the first place.

We call this "The Classic Game" and the Classic Game is

endless, it is extremely powerful and as you will find out, the key that unlocks all your magic in the end, quite practically.

Here is how it works.

The Classic Game

We will use the symbols to take us to the right place in time and space where we can find what we are looking for.

We use the following symbols to accomplish this:

1. Space

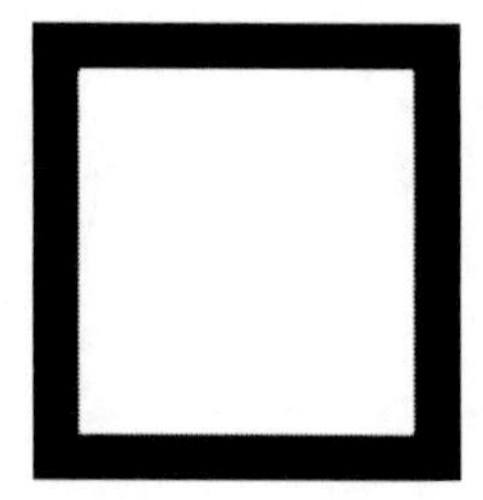

This is the travelling instruction for the energy mind to take us "somewhere" on this occasion, and where we want to go is being placed upfront, using the following instruction:

"Take me to the perfect place
in time and space ..."

... where I can meet my Guardian Angel

... where I can find a spell for Uncle Peter

... where I can consult with my power animal

... where I will find the right artefact for this ritual I'm working on

... where I can observe the stars to complete my astrological chart

... where I can meet the spirit of my dead ancestors

... and so on and so on, ad infinitum.

This simple, basic set up of the Classic Game keeps you safe, keeps you on track, and it literally does "take you to the perfect place in time and space" where those things you seek, can be found, realistically and practically.

Just for a moment, take a mental step back and think about that.

With that one simple instruction you have taken control of your travel in the other worlds, in the other realms; and if it can be done at all, your energy mind, working in conjunction with all your helpful spirits, your higher aspects, your soul, your guardian angels and your highest path itself WILL TAKE YOU THERE WITHOUT A FAIL.

There has never been anything even remotely like it in the history of witchcraft (by any other name); nothing as simple, nothing as direct, and nothing as powerful.

What we are looking at here, and what you will EXPERIENCE when you use this movement of consciousness, is simply an example of working WITH the gifts the Creative Order gave each one of us, by virtue of design.

We are magical designs, and if we use ourselves correctly, we can do things and know things that likewise, the world has never known or seen before.

The next step in the Classic Game, after we have stated what we are seeking in the set up, the travel instructions, is to find our way to that exact perfect place in time and space.

2. Time

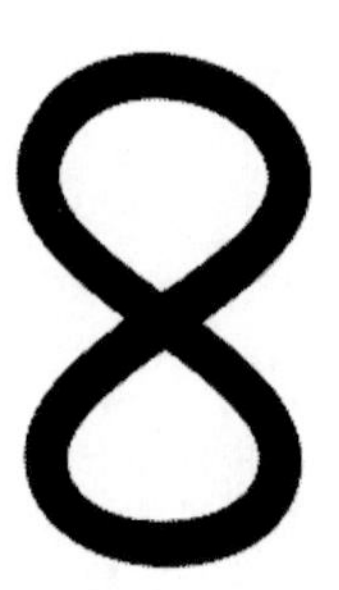

We do this by using the Time symbol next, and we ask, "What is the time of day? What is the time of year?"

Our energy mind will send us a vision (which remember, is not just visual, but much more importantly, feelings, things we hear, sensations and knowings too) which will answer that question.

As an example, let us say I asked today, "Take me to the perfect place in time and space to meet a Guardian Angel I have never known before."

As I consider the time, I find it is very early morning, just after dawn, and it is early summer here in this "perfect place in time and space".

3. Weather

The next question is: What is the weather here?

In my example, the weather is incredibly perfect, fine and clear, fresh morning air and the sky is the most wonderful shade of radiant blue. The sun is young and loving still, warm without hurting my skin or being a danger in any way, and a perfect day early summer's day lies ahead from here.

4. The Land

What is the landscape here?

With every question answered, attention paid to this perfect place in time and space, more information becomes revealed and this place becomes more and more real, as more and more sensory information is added and our consciousness steps across and into that place more perfectly still.

My landscape is a grassy valley with low hills; soft grasses that move in the morning wind, and to the right I can just see the silver shimmer of an ocean, or a very large lake at the horizon.

5. The Plants

What kinds of plants exist here?

There are the grasses, but in the grasses live many other forms of plants; there are small herbs and many flowers, sparkling little colours in the sunlight that look like little stars scattered across the valley.

6. The Animals

What kinds of animals exist here?

Small life forms in the grass, and further away there are herds of grazing animals. Above, I can see large birds but they are very, very high above indeed.

In this example, I have found the place in space and time and I am there. Now, I can go ahead and meet my Guardian Angel there; if there is any further action required from me, I can use the symbols to further the story and ask, **"What happens next?"**

So this is "The Classic Game" and your most important practice piece to start making connections with the other realms, with dreamtime, the spirit world and the many dimensions in which we may travel freely.

If you are new to magic, I recommend you find yourself a friend first of all, someone you can communicate with and who can help you decide what steps you want to take and in which order.

If you already have a spirit guide, meet them in "the perfect place in time and space" to have an experience of the directness and clarity of conversing with friends and guides in this way.

- **Remember: The more attention you can pay to your guide, the more you can love them, the more perfect the relationship will be and the more YOU will get out of this in every way.**

There is every merit in taking time to get to know your guides VERY well; ask them questions about their homelands, their other lives, what their favourite colour is, what they like to eat, and also go on journeys and quests together, much like you would go on an adventure date to find out more about a potential life partner.

Likewise, there is merit in inviting a guide to your home and life in the hard and show them around; the more they know about you, the better they can help you out.

Now, I recommend that you undertake the following journeys as exercises, one at a time, to give you forward momentum in the development of your magic power.

The Magical Self Within

Meet with your magical self and let them show you a special place where you can come and get advice on all magical things.

Give your magical self a The Gift and receive one in return.

Over the next three days, return three times (so the path is clear) give and receive a further three gifts which will help you get closer to your magical self, and improve your magic sense and magic power.

"Take me to the perfect place in time and space where I will meet my magical self."

Your Magic Central

It is good at the beginning to make a special habitat that is your "magic central" and contains lots of things you need for your magic.

It is clearly going to be a specially protected space with many features a magician needs, and you can build more over time.

Here, you can also perform more complex rituals, using very large circles and installations as space, time and resources are no object here.

Creating your own first "magic central" is a FANTASTIC experience, full of wonders and surprises. It teaches you lots and lots about yourself and you end up with this fabulous place where you can do serious magic, but also just have a good time if you want.

Remember that you don't have to make it up, but that you can use the symbols to help you create the perfect dwelling, find the right artefacts, have support from spirit animals, a healing garden, crystal forms and installations, a planetarium perhaps and whatever else you need to set your magic self free to learn about the Universe.

"Take me to the perfect place in time and space where I can build my magic home."

The Magic Quest

Let yourself be shown to a realm where some of your missing magic can be found.

Go on a quest and take as many friends and helpers as you need to recover your missing magic.

"Take me to the perfect place in time and space where I can find my missing magic."

Your Magic Name

Traditionally, magicians have many different names and most of them are unknown to other people.

A magic name, or another magic name if you know one already, adds new aspects to your concept as a magical being and is a method by which we can unlock new powers and new directions.

This is a journey you can take often, and I recommend doing this once a year, to help you evolve your magical persona and not get stuck on a single track when there is so much room for growth and exploration.

"Take me to the perfect place in time and space where I can discover a new magical name."

Healing Domains

It is very important for someone who starts using their magic powers to look after themselves magically speaking. We use a lot of energies and most of us don't have "the perfect energy system" that can handle all of that perfectly well. Especially at the beginning.

So it is important to take time out and visit with a land, a domain or a realm that gives you the right energies back to help you rebalance and find your Even Flow.

There are infinite realms out there for you to draw energy and healing from, restoration and rejuvenation, more love and more power overall; so don't get stuck in one or two domains, but find THE RIGHT ONE for THIS ONE DAY, the one that is truly perfect in every way to do the best that can be done for you.

That way, you get to experience many, many different domains and you get lots of different "energy vitamins" as and when you need them.

Make it a habit to visit one of these healing domains at least once a day, before you go to sleep at night, or after any very heavy duty piece of magic work so you learn how it works and you can get there easily, and any time you need it.

Meeting Helpful Spirits

In the past, all manner of spirits were called to the same place; some might like that, but for others it is less than comfortable. Working with the infinite domains, we always put up front:

"Take me to the perfect place in time and space where I can meet ..."

- my ancestors
- my guardian angel
- my higher self
- a representative of my soul
- the spirit of the animal kingdom
- the spirit of water
- a new spirit guide
- my ex-boyfriend's higher self
- my spirit animal guide
- a new friend
- someone I really need to listen to right now.

Work your way through this list for practice and notice how the environments, the domains and dimensions play such an important part in how the meeting goes, and what you bring back from the meeting.

Soul Piloting

In magic, we are pretty much constantly asking for help from the spirit world, from here, there, and everywhere.

Soul Piloting is a way in which we can give back to the spirit world, a gift of our own uniqueness and to some good.

In short, travel to a domain or dimension where you will meet a lost soul, and you will help them find their way back to their own path - to the light, or wherever they need to go.

Lost souls get "stuck" in strange ways and in strange places, and if no-one comes to help them, eventually they erode away, become brittle and dry and disintegrate, and then all they ever were is lost to all of us.

Lost souls have all different frequencies, and they can't be reached by the higher beings which have very fine frequencies. Us lot down here, who are still half earthbound and with all the various problems and individual set ups that we have, are similar to them and we can reach them.

Each one of us will find souls that are the perfect match to ourselves at this time, and in helping the lost souls, not only do you give back to the Universe itself, but you also learn a lot about the ways of magic, life and death so it is good for you too.

Each soul you help on its path gives you a gift too - a message, a learning, an energy, an understanding, a loving and much more besides.

I recommend Soul Piloting strongly for anyone who wants to do good with their magic and become a well rounded magical person.

"Take me to the perfect time and place where a lost soul needs my help."

The Magical Child Within

Meeting your magical child within, getting to know it, playing and dancing with it is a source of great joy, of great reconnection, and a particularly wonderful form of true light magic.

There are many frequencies to our magic, like there are uncountable colours in a rainbow, and more of these frequencies we can activate, the richer and more powerful as a magical person we become.

In the olden days, especially men would practice dour and repetitive forms of what they thought was magic, involving numbers and charts and demons and much dust of the ages. These people were clearly missing the vibration of the magical child within, their rainbow being permanently stuck on midnight and on ultra-violet, and thus neither being beautiful, nor in any sense of the word, COMPLETE.

"Take me to the perfect time and place where I can meet my magical child within."

Remember to give lots of The Gifts - and receive lots, too! These can become wonderful toys for you to play with, to experience lightness and delight in magic which is SO important in all your dealings with nature and the higher beings, and which makes magic instead of boring, dour and spooky, delightful, powerful and as attractive as the most beautifully sparkling diamond in the sunshine!

The Magical Demon Within

A proper rainbow wouldn't be a rainbow without the ultraviolet side of things. Don't be afraid of the magical demon within; it was fear, terror and confusion which made people in the Middle Ages beat themselves senseless with sticks and hallucinate endlessly about devils and all of that.

Yes, people do have a shadow side, and no, that's not evil, it's the shadow side!

There, things are different; but the shadow side is still a part of the Universe, and the Universe is beautiful, holy, logical and amazing.

The shadow side likewise is amazing - it sometimes seems alien, and people who stumbled into other cultures from way back when obviously saw "devils" everywhere, but we do know better than that these days.

Use EmoTrance to soften and flow your fears away so that your energy runs cleanly and observe the shadow side, observe and meet your magical demon within without fear, without prejudice.

It may be alien and other than, to be sure, but you will find that it is beautiful, and holds a special kind of power, and brings the ultraviolet dimensions into your magical rainbow for you need to know them, understand them, and be able to use them to deal with

REALITY correctly.

"Take me to the perfect time and place where I can meet my magical demon within."

Spiritualism

The Sanctuary realms are THE perfect place to meet with dead ancestors, dead family members, and other dead people's spirits that might help in what you are trying to achieve.

As there are a lot of spirits around, you need to be precise when you want to use the spirit world in the sense of using the support of people who are on the other side for a project such as a spell, a ritual or in general, what you want to get done on this occasion.

People who go round saying, "I want to hear dead people ..." get overwhelmed with the voices and the chatter; this is not helpful, so be very specific.

"Take me to the perfect time and place where I can meet a spirit (or a group of spirits) who will assist me with winning the court case against X."

"Take me to the perfect time and place where I can meet with the spirit of my mother so she can assist with the birth of her great grand daughter, my grandchild."

"Take me to the perfect time and place where I will meet the right spirit who has information on the disappearance of Y."

If you are doing spiritualism on behalf of other people, likewise phrase it tightly and specifically:

"Take me to the perfect time and place where I will meet with a spirit who has an important message for Anne about her illness today."

"Take me to the perfect time and place where I can meet Anne's father so she can ask him some questions."

"Take me to the perfect time and place where I can find out if Anne's father has made it into the spirit world ok, and found Anne's mother and his brother there."

As you can tell, instead of getting the spirits to come "into the room" here, we meet them half way. This is MUCH safer, MUCH more successful, much easier on the spirits, and leads to much clearer and more precise information being brought back to the querent.

Additionally, the domain where we meet the spirit is often soothing to the querent. They might recognise it or it might be very relevant to the person who passed over. For example; Anne's father had been a navy captain and the place where we went to meet him was by a sea shore.

If you have never practised spiritualism before, I recommend you try it because it is a special skill that belongs firmly into what magical people can do.

Spiritualism is extremely useful, not just after bereavements to bring peace of mind to the grieving. The spirit world is full of people who are dying to help us out (pardon the pun!) and would LOVE to give us advice, energy, insights if only we met them half way and thought to ask, once in a while.

Exploring Your Magical Heritage

It is completely fascinating to meet with members of your extended ancestry who are your magical heritage in Sanctuary. Often people think they're one thing, or another - black or white, for example, or Greek, or Roman.

But people have been making love and making babies across cultural, racial and societal divides for as long as there have been human beings on this planet.

Not only that, "Witchy" people have always sought and found each other in preference to creed, race or colour, so even though you may think that your magical heritage is "pure Celtic" or "pure Romany" or "pure Voodoo" that's usually far from the truth.

There are MANY magical heritages awaiting your discovery. Go back a few hundred generations and what might you find?

Re-connecting with the many lines of your true magical heritage across the ages is just amazing, and it enriches your magic practice enormously.

I can tell you from personal experience that I've rarely been so delighted, so excited or so uplifted than by discovering a magical heritage I never knew I had, meeting with those ancestors, being welcomed by them, and being supported by them now.

"Take me to the perfect time and place to meet magical ancestors I never knew I had!"

Past Life Regression

Magical people and past lives are like leaves and trees - you rarely meet one without the other being somewhere in the neighbourhood!

There is a theory that in order to manifest magic in THIS life, you have had to have had quite a few lives under your belt already in the first place.

I don't know if this is strictly true, but to meet with past life selves and to do something with those past life memories is an extremely enriching experience.

Many magical people had past lives where they were badly treated BECAUSE they were magical people.

This resonates down through the soul line into our current lives and accounts for much of the fear, terror, and inexplicable sense of paranoia many magical people experience today.

By travelling back to a past self, let's say one that was tortured and then burned at the stake for being a witch, and making that life and death more peaceful by the application of magic can be a wonderful boost for the flowering of magical abilities in THIS life.

You can for example take the spirit of a person out of the body that is being tortured and hold them close and tight, so they feel no pain and they understand that all of that is over now, and that they played an amazing part in your joined soul's journey. You can tell them of your gratitude to them, and take them to "the perfect place in space and time" where they can rest and be happy, and heal of the scars of that life absolutely.

Then when they are ready, they can re-join your soul group and be a shining star and a super-powerful resource for you in this life, and for all the other lives that know no linear time, as well.

Past life regression is not just about finding tortured souls; it can be about anything really, and you can trust that your higher self will point you in the right direction, and for your highest good, when you ask,

"Take me to the perfect place in time and space to meet a past self that needs my help today."

"Take me to the perfect place in time and space where I can meet a past self that holds the key to (...) today."

"Take me to the perfect place in time and space to meet a past self that can help me with (...) today."

Saving The Evil Magicians & Witches

Finally, on the past lives topic I would also like to mention that many current magical people have "evil magicians" in their soul line.

By that I mean not evil in the "ooh! it's so evil!" sense but simply ordinary people who may have misused their magical powers and found out later that they created pain, suffering, and chaos for themselves and others as a result.

These people then decided, in their guilt and shame, that they were evil and put a block on their magic, and unknowingly so, also on the magic of their soul line from that moment forth.

We all make mistakes, and nobody is perfect. It just often happens that out of not knowing terrible things can arise; magical people get angry when they are hurt and hurl back dreadful revenge in a moment of high disturbance, and it is important for an active magical person today to seek out such past selves in the soul line and find a way for them to be given, and to accept, absolution for their "magical sins" whatever they may have been.

- **In the Universe of light, all is forgivable; there is no sin so great that the force of love won't wash it away in an instance if there is a**

readiness to accept that, and embrace that, and make it become a living reality in you today.

This is very powerful stuff, but you can trust your own magic, your own guides and supporting spirits, and most of all, your higher self to guide you in the right direction when you ask:

"Take me to a place in time and space where I can save a past self who still thinks they are evil."

The Classic Game In Overview

The Classic Game, that will take you to the right place in time and space where you can learn, explore, and practice your magic skills in safety and with so much support, is in and of itself never ending.

But it is even more important than that.

Every time you play the Classic Game, every single time you take a journey to one of these many realms and step into your magical self there, interact, talk, communicate, heal, fight, make love there something quite extraordinary happens.

The magic realms come CLOSER to the hard of every day.

You will find that ALL your magic skills across the board begin to improve.

Your sense and awareness of what objects mean, of what lies behind the masks of symbols and of words will become much, much more acute.

You will find that your personal power and attractiveness rises – your X-Factor increases dramatically.

You will find that your natural knowing and your natural talents come to the fore much more readily, and you will be able to spot "invitations to magic" as and when they arise.

As this is such an important part of becoming a truly great magician, I would like to take a moment now and tell you about "the magic of the moment".

THE MAGIC OF THE MOMENT

The most powerful of all spells and rituals are not what you plot and plan for month on end and make a great big effort over – amazingly, the most powerful magic happens "in the moment".

You can think of this like people plan these huge and super-expensive weddings, and they are alright and will produce photographs and such, but when you ask the bride after 40 years of marriage what she remembers, she will say it was that day at the boat yard, and she got scared by a big crab someone was waving about, and her husband took her in his arms and made her feel safe and it was so incredibly romantic and wonderful, she's never forgotten it.

In a million years you couldn't plan for something as peculiar as some guy waving a crab around at a boat yard; this is true magic of the moment.

There are invitations to magic all around us; they exist in every day, and come in so many different forms.

The best way I can explain this is to give you some of my favourite "magic of the moment" experiences.

There was one day where my son spotted we had a heart shaped potato in the bag; it was Mother's Sunday on that day as well and so we made a little spontaneous ritual that was truly delightful, right there and then.

There was one day where I was at the supermarket and as I came out, I saw the incredibly sharp divide between the shadow from the roof and the sunlight beyond. I made a spell as I stepped across the divide that I would always seek the light, live in the light. It was simply amazing.

There was one day in spring when I parked in town and saw this huge, huge cherry tree in full blossom. I connected with it and took some of its petals, knowing that they would make a different kind of perfect love spell that contained the power of spring, eternal youth and true cycles of life within it. It was a perfect "magic moment".

There was a time when I was sitting outside a hotel in a strange country and I saw a beggar go by. There was a moment and I knew it and I blessed the beggar and then, the whole town and everyone in it; it was such a profound experience from my end, I nearly fainted; I have rarely done such powerful magic or raised such powerful energies.

When my children were small, a bird got trapped in our bathroom. It was hysterical and hurting itself against the windows. I charmed it and it became so calm, I could gently pick it up and then let it fly out of the window. A small piece of magic, but when I turned around I saw both my kids looking at me with these big, wide eyes and I knew they had learned something about magic on this day.

These are not "great rituals" to raise a million devils and demons. They are little things but they are truly magical; and it is in these "little spells" and having the magic around you, close to you, inviting you to take action that the skills, experience and confidence in one's own magical abilities arise. When it then comes to the "great big rituals" then they too become a different experience, lifted by all these incidences of small magic and the true magic of the moment.

Creating Magical Tools

There are two kinds of magical tools.

The first kind only exists in Sanctuary, at the level and in the domains of the energy dimensions.

I would point out that such magical tools can be a lot more powerful than those which are the second kind, those which exist in Sanctuary AND in the hard at the same time, because there are no restrictions whatsoever upon those tools, and you can shape them, build them and empower and evolve them further over time.

It is extremely important for any magician to learn to take the energy levels really seriously and don't rate them as second best to the level at which rocks fall on your head. This is a classic entrainment we all have inherited from our lives within our various societies and one that we must strive to overcome.

In the creation of magical tools, we have an opportunity to practice giving equal attention and love to both kinds of tools, and not think one to be better or more effective than another.

The Magic Wand

One of the most primal and basic magic tools is the magic wand, or in other words, a stick.

Using a stick to reach something that you can't quite reach with your hands alone is the first active and conscious form of tool usage; so when we make ourselves a stick we call a magic wand, we are going right back to the basics of human endeavour and we connect with the most primal form of magic, one that precedes making fire by millennia (!).

For this exercise, let us make two magic wands - one which will exist only on the level of energy, and the second which will exist on the levels of energy AND in the hard.

We are going to use the Classic Game first of all to show us how we need to proceed for the first magic wand.

"Take me to the perfect place in time and space where I can discover my magic wand of energy."

Take the journey, discover your new energy magic wand, and take it to your "magic central" world to have in your house there, and to use it in any spell casting or ceremony at that level you might want to undertake.

Now, we can use the Classic Game to make the second

magic wand and we ask:

"Take me to the perfect place in time and space where I can learn what I need to learn to find my perfect magic wand to use both in the energy realms, and in the hard."

This vision will show you what you need to do in order to make a magic wand you can hold in your physical hands.

It will show you what kind of wood you need, what kind of tree, where to find this, and how to decorate and prepare your magic wand.

When you follow the course of action that is outlined for you, in this instance have yourself be both in your magic home AND in your hard home at the same time, taking the same actions AT THE SAME TIME, so the resulting object is existent on both levels, and in a manner of speaking, binds these levels together.

- **A note: If your vision shows you something that you can't possibly make happen in the hard, such as taking the top branch from some unknown tree that grows only in the heart of the Amazonian rain forest, and there's no way you can afford the expedition costs and airplane tickets, refine your request and ask for something that you can achieve right here and now.**

You may find that there is a tree in your garden, growing just down the street or round the corner which will yield your stick that will become a magic wand.

Using The Magic Wand

In cartoons and movies, magic wands shoot energy out of them like a laser gun, and that is certainly one way of using one, to focus energy onto a fine point or in a wide spray, in a nice and symmetrical fashion.

A magic wand can also function the other way around, however, as an amplifier to bring energies into your system so that you can feel them more easily.

Learning to feel energy forms and to be able to tell when they are coming into alignment is a key skill of working with all forms of magic; some people call this "intuition" but what it is to feel energy forms through your body.

As an exercise, take your new magic wand and direct it towards one of the symbols. Let it draw that energy into you in that amplified, focused fashion which magic wands produce by nature and notice how this feels.

If you have any problems with this amplified energy, it hurts somewhere in your body or causes feelings of discomfort, use the Clearing the Path exercise to make sure you get a clean and delicious energy flow in, through and out of yourself.

Try the wand in the left and the right hand, and in both together to note the difference.

Another good beginner's exercise is to draw the symbols into the air using the magic wand. You will notice that the portals you create in that way are quite different in nature, due to the wand's amplification action; and they stand very sharp and clear as a result.

A magic wand is an interesting magical tool you can do many things with, but I would also advise you to remember that you have (normally) ten fingers which are all magic wands in their own right, and that's something you take with you where ever you go, you can't lose them, and that's most direct form of energy transmission, and the most natural one.

Using The Energy Wand In Sanctuary

The "energy only" wand in Sanctuary is primarily a training aid to make you understand how you can paint, touch, create, move and influence energetic realities with a magic wand.

Here, you can make the influences of the magic wand visible and you can practice making patterns and grids, making connections and changes and you can see this playing out in shapes and forms of light.

In Sanctuary also, you can make the kind of transformations that you can see in the cartoons - you could there, if you would choose to do such a thing, transform a person's human spirit into a pig spirit, or a mouse spirit and significantly influence their existence in that way.

I highly recommend you seek guidance before you do something like that; it is not a first choice and the situations where one might want to do such a thing are rather rare.

Using your energy wand in Sanctuary can give you important information about how to work a wand in general and teach you lessons about its usage and powers that you can't learn in any other way; so take it with you as you go about your journeys of exploration and use it so you gain maximum experience with the oldest tool of them all.

The Descendants Of The Magic Wand

The magic wand has many descendants; amongst those are knives, spears, swords, arrows, pistols, guns and bombs, and on another developmental line, we have pencils, paint brushes, printing presses, typewriters and even computer keyboards.

There is a developmental line of the old magic wand which contains string, ribbon, chain and thread which eventually turns into woven cloth and fabrics; and the heritage of tools from stick to screw driver, ratchet, hammer, spoon and fork.

All of those are objects that extend a person's ability to touch reality; all of those can be turned into their own version of "magic wands" much in the same way as a simple stick becomes just that.

Once you understand this basic principle, you can choose your magic tools according to their purpose and according to YOUR NEEDS, rather than any form of traditional approach that may or may not feel right to you, and may or may not make sense to you.

It opens the world of magical tools to you in a very profound and personal way; and the tools of YOUR trade can then become, quite practically, your magic wands that do not just affect that which can be seen, but all the levels and layers beyond.

Magic Stones

The second oldest form of magic known to human kind is the magic of stones.

In a way, we are evoking this exact form of magic when we are creating our own personal Stonehenge using the symbols on their markers, and we are connecting with this hugely powerful, primal form of pure magic.

The stone becomes a "stand in" for something else; a portal through which intention may travel to something else.

For example, one of the oldest, simplest and most profound forms of distance healing involves nothing more than to dedicate a stone to a person; so it becomes a portal to that person and what energies you address to that stone, is transferred to that person.

The Healing Stone Exercise

Take a simple stone, such as you find in a field or on a country road, or near a river bed.

Dedicate the stone to a person you want to send your love to by holding it in your hands, saying the person's name, and sealing it with a kiss.

Now hold the stone to your heart and let your flow into the stone; by definition through the stone that has become the portal, TO that person you want to bless with your heart's love.

If you do it right, this will be an immensely emotional experience; you have created a real magic event and there will be knowing of this action, and results, because you have changed the world.

Real magic is as simple as this, and as profound as this.

Learn how to do these simple, basic, primal things well; reconnect to your abilities to feel and direct your attention with love and the greatest known challenges of magic become easy in turn.

PLEASE do not let the sheer simplicity of something like this stone healing spell fool you into thinking that this isn't as "good" as some complicated ritual that takes a month to prepare, and includes ten thousand items, chants, grids, charts and all the rest of it.

The chances that you can do real good with something as simple as this stone healing spell are much, much higher because every extra step added to a spell, every extra ingredient added to a potion, every extra twist, turn, symbol or chant in a ritual makes it more diffuse and adds the possibility of noise and disturbance creeping in.

In the magic worlds, more is NOT always better; and in fact the less there is, the less there can go wrong with it, and more powerfully aligned it is BY DESIGN and definition.

Single stone portals can be made to and for everything, not just people; but it is especially with people that these stone portals are particularly effective.

You can make beautifully complex magic with a few simple stones, good intention and your heart in the right place. Here are just two simple examples.

Making A Family Grid

Gather some stones to represent a family, one stone per person.

If you want to, and this can be helpful to beginners, write the name of the person on the stone, or their initial.

Now place these stones on the table in front of you, and move them around so that they have the correct relationship to each other.

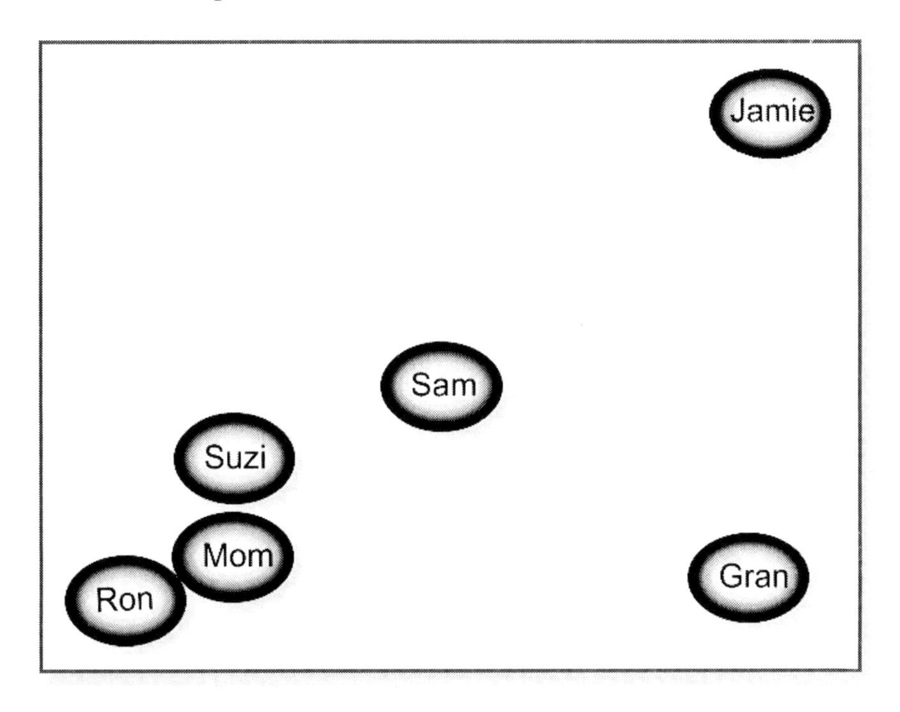

You can't do this consciously. You have to use the "FEEL the magic!" exercise for this and listen with your fingertips and with your whole body for that "cold, warm, hot – CLICK! That's the right place!" experience. This will tell you exactly where is the right place for that stone to go in the grid.

When the family grid is right, and lies in front of you, you can now act on that whole family in many different magical ways.

You can:

- Bless the entire grid;
- Create a circle of protection and safety around them;
- Remove bad luck and family curses;
- Move some members of that family into another (better) position to each other;
- Find the "black sheep" and give them special love and healing;
- Evoke prosperity energy for this family;

... and anything else you would like to do that influences the family system as a whole.

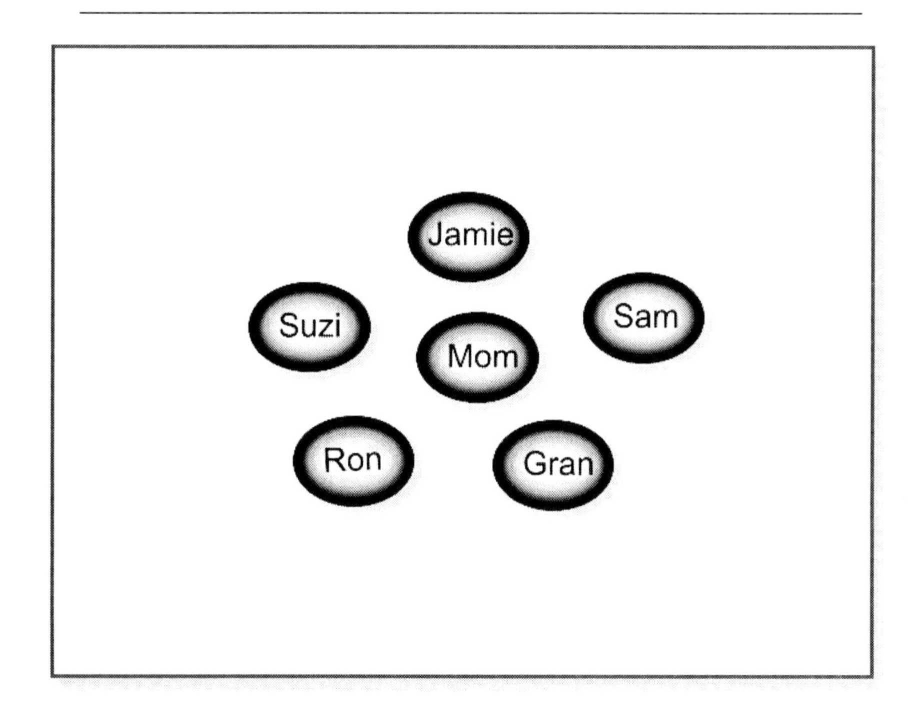

- **Stone magic is HUGELY powerful magic, even in the hands of a complete beginner.**

I would also point out that any system that is made up out of numerous components can be magically dealt with in this way; a company, for example; a group of animals; a group of friends; a rock band; a band of brothers; divisions within a company, and any other such system you might want to affect at the magic levels.

Counting Your Blessings

Counting stones is nearly as old as stone magic and humanity itself; here is a very beautiful, simple and profound ritual that you can do for yourself, or with someone else to raise your level of blessings, raise your spirits, and help you find the true magic in your life.

Find a hundred small stones or anything that can serve as a stone on this occasion.

Place them on the left hand side of the table.

On the right hand side of the table, draw a circle with your fingertip and write your name inside.

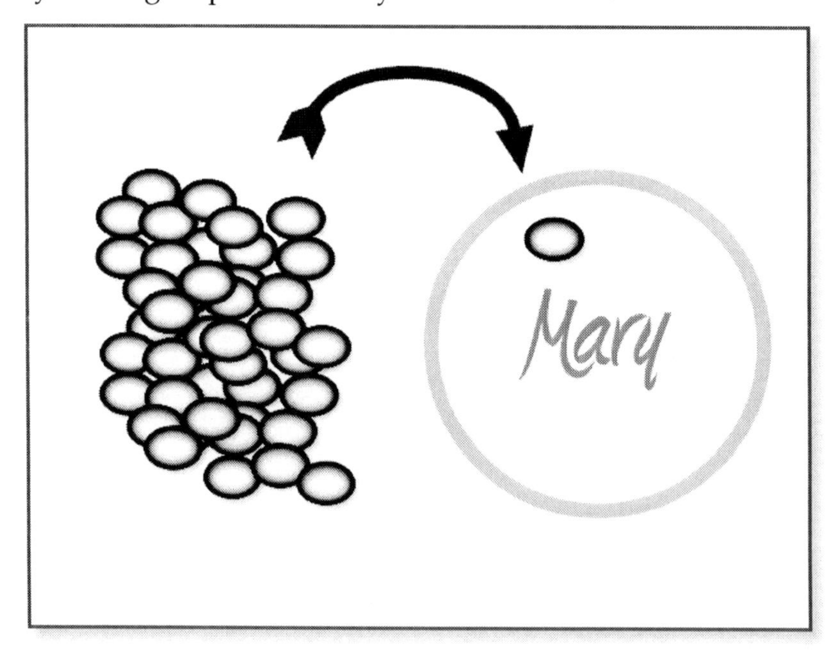

Now pick up the first stone and think of a blessing you have been given; for example, "I am blessed with good health." - "I am blessed with having a wonderful cat that loves me." - "I am blessed with the power of speech." - whatever comes to mind and in no particular order.

Put the blessing into the circle that is you.

Continue until all 100 blessings have been received by you.

Then, hold your hands over the whole lot and draw the energy of ALL OF THAT into yourself all at once to create that true "magic event" that really makes you tingle through and through.

Thank the stones, the powers that be and yourself and enjoy!

The Descendants Of Stone Magic

Clearly, all forms of divination in use today, be it shamanic bones on a drum; Tarot cards; runes; playing cards, and our own Genius Symbols are all descendants of stone magic.

Also, all forms of lettering, numbering and counting come from stone magic and making shapes and patterns from stones.

What is also directly related to stone magic is the making of statues of animals, and particularly of people. The poppets from traditional witchcraft which are used to form a portal to a person work in exactly that way; and they evolve from marking the stone with a symbol, or a face, personalising it with a strand of hair perhaps; and all this evolves into making fully fledged marble sculptures of the saints, or huge statues of the Buddha.

Making totems to be portals to animal spirits comes from the same developmental line; and so does cave paintings which then develop into all the various forms of human drawing and painting, technical as well as artistically - and on into photography, cinematography, and even acting where the actor become "the stone that is the portal to" another being or another person.

One should also mention that all forms of adornment,

jewellery, and of course, coins and money derive from the stones just the same.

When you connect with the primal power and original idea of using a stone for a portal that gives you access to the "inner programming" of someone or some thing else, you regain at the same time the power over all writing, symbols, numbers, over money and over essential human artistic expression.

That is a very wonderful thing, and allows you as a magical person to have a safe platform to which you can return, should you get ever lost or confused along the way.

Water Magic

Water is THE one and only original magic potion.

Whatever else you do, and whatever else you might add to it, in the end it comes down to the very existence of water where the real magic happens.

In space exploration, it is the presence of water that is held to be the key to life itself; without it, there is no life as we know it.

Through the water cycle, the water in our own bodies connects us with everything else there ever was, even to comets that came from the sky and brought their water with them and that is now mixed up with all the water that exists on Planet Earth.

You can "immerse" yourself in endless recipes for this, that and the other; but in the end, it is the water, the wisdom of the water, and the incredible magic power inherent in a single drop even that drives all magic potions.

Imprinting Water

The most pure, simple and once again, profound form of potion making is to imprint water with magic intention.

People who don't understand and can't feel energy and magic really do not understand this one and use particularly this as an example how "mad" people who do practice magic actually are.

For example, we might write the name of a person on a piece of paper with a pen (a descendent of the magic wand, inscribing this portal in symbols which are the descendants of the original stone portals) and then place a glass of water on top of this piece of paper with the name on it.

We may then ask for a "perfect potion to heal (name) of (problem)" and leave the water there for one sunshine day and one moonlit night; then we might put this in a bottle, seal it with wax, and give this magic potion to that person.

The "scientist" runs off into their laboratory, examines the "chemical properties" of the water and finds – nothing.

They happily conclude that there is no such thing as magic and all this bottle contained was nothing more than "just water".

Oh ye of little ... no, not faith. Oh ye of little energy

intelligence, magical talent, intuition, and simple common sense. It's sad, really ...

However, there are aspects in all of us modern human beings who have been tainted with this idea that if you can't measure it, it cannot exist.

Some scientists are back-pedalling on that one; the astrophysicists talk of the material Universe consisting of 90% "dark matter" aka stuff they don't know what it is, can't see, can't measure, but that, if it wasn't there, nothing would make any sense at all.

Any person who works with magic must learn to overcome their own doubts and devise for themselves experiments that will prove to themselves BEYOND ALL REASONALBE DOUBT that their magic water really IS magic and that is really DOES work.

In order to conduct those experiments, you have to start DOING THINGS – you have to practice. There is no shortcut to that; you can't go on EBay and buy the "advanced manual on especially insane and dangerous demons," read that and short circuit the practice in that way. In fact, all you do if you try is to waste your time, fill your head with even more nonsense, and get nowhere, slowly, at that.

Here are some ideas how to practice with magic water and learn how it is not just extremely real, but extremely powerful. We are NOT going to conduct experiments with negative vibrations or destructive energies; there's quite enough of that to go around already. What we will do instead is to compare water that was not treated, with water that was turned into a magic potion and compare the results.

You can use as your experimental group any kind of living being in your environment you have ready access to. Some people have a lot of children; some have a lot of dogs, cats or fish; some have house plants; but everyone has some form of life in their environment they can use to test the magic potions.

Very simply and as an example, choose four house plants. Water two with magic water that has been imprinted with love and extra life force energy; and the other two with "normal" water of the same temperature and amount.

Within a short time, you will be able to see the difference between the blessed group, and the control group, quite practically, measurably and absolutely.

If you did this in a hospital with patients, your statistics would show the same results; and that is simply a fact and something science calls "the placebo effect" only just how pets, farm animals, fish and houseplants can "imagine themselves better" is apparently still quite undiscovered ...

Once you can wholeheartedly embrace the concept of magic water, you have "cleared the paths" of doubt and fear (including the fear of what would happen if it really did work, and work reliably, and miraculously, every time!) you have a resource on your hands that is quite amazing in its capacity to do good.

As long as you have water, you have magic potions – in all vibrations, in every way, even if you don't have a single herb or chemical in your possession that you can add to the water.

The water becomes your blank canvas upon which you can imprint truly elegant and wondrous levels and layers of intention and energy; this is the art in magic as you tune into someone or some thing, hold it clear in your mind what you want to give them, be steady in your heart and use the magic of your soul to create the potions of the ages – beautiful, resonant, and so very, very powerful in the true sense of the word.

Imprinting Water Using The Gift Exercise

Get a nice and magical bottle for this purpose; use the CLICK! to choose just the right one for this purpose, for this person or animal, on this occasion.

Fill the bottle with water from any safe drinking water source.

Hold the bottle to your heart and close your eyes.

Now let a The Gift come to you; know it completely and feel that energy beginning to gather inside you as you raise the energy of The Gift.

When it fills you to overflowing and you can't hold it any longer, discharge this energy like a lightning strike into the water.

Seal the bottle with a kiss and give it to the recipient, to add three drops a day to their drinks for 3x3 days.

As Long As There Is Water ...

I would like to mention that as long as there is water, you can use it to make a magic potion out of it. A bottle of beer or wine; vodka, milk, in fact any drink of any kind leads itself to carry the message of the water.

Soup, gravy, and especially fruit contain lots of water and as you practice the basic transfer of The Gifts and other energy forms into water receptors, you will also get a lot faster at it.

So remember – when a real energy magician brings you a bunch of grapes in hospital to help you get better, eat them with care and gratitude, and note how they make you feel, a single grape at a time.

Natural Healing Water

Every so often you come across a well, spring or body of water that has natural healing properties; a naturally occurring vibration and set of energy forms that makes it particularly beneficial for healing, wish fulfilment, prosperity and so forth.

When you come across this, and these kinds of waters are not always found just in "holy" places where all the non-magical folk queue up and hope for the best, and your newfound energy spider sense starts to tingle, make good use of the opportunity that presents itself there.

You should collect such water because this baseline, natural imprint that comes from the circumstances of Mother Earth herself is priceless and will lift whatever you then add to it to new levels.

Rain falling on special days and in special circumstances can serve a similar purpose.

There is a lot of water about, and to tune into that, and work with it, is a core skill for any magician and it is also one where you don't just "learn it" and that's all there is, but where you can develop true virtuosity and levels of mastery as your magic grows.

FIRE MAGIC

The last of the truly primal magic of humanity is that which eventually changed everything; how to make a fire and fire magic.

When you work with fire magic you really do travel across time and space to a particular time in human development in your own ancestry. A pivotal moment indeed.

What is so fascinating about fire is that it is bright, and brings light to the night; it is hot, and it destroys the physical form of things.

It is in that movement that fire magic has its most powerful applications; namely to transfer intent to the powers that be by destroying the physical form, leaving the energy form free to take flight and become independent, to act independently, not being earthbound any longer.

Writing A Letter To The Powers That Be Exercise

For this exercise, write a short letter to the powers that be (all your helpful spirits and guardians, known and unknown alike) and ask them to do something for you.

You could ask them for a specific sign, or a surprise; or to do anything magical on your behalf.

Please AVOID asking for some mundane thing that you can get from a cheap shopping catalogue or department store; the usual muppet thing of "winning the lottery" or such like nonsense that is as disrespectful to the powers that be as it is indicative of a really small mind in the querent just the same.

Ask for something that would really take a miracle to achieve, or something that money can't buy, or that can't buy you money; only then can you be sure you are dealing really with the powers that be and not an accident or coincidence, one way or the other.

Write the letter respectfully and in your best handwriting, on your best paper and with your best pen. Put it in an envelope and address it "To the Powers That Be".

Find a suitably peaceful time, light a fire with wood in a safe way and hold the letter in your hand, contemplating the request, contemplating how the symbols you wrote on the paper with your magic wand/pen are holding the message at this time energetically as well as physically.

Now say to yourself and say in your mind:

"Powers that be,

hear me, heed me.

This request from me

to thee, this is my will,

so will it be."

This little rhyme is much more for you than it is for the powers who are generally looking in and listening all the time; and it helps you move into the right state to make that transfer request that will release the energy form from the letter, let it take wing and make its way like an official document of request to the powers that be.

When you are ready, kiss the letter and put it in the fire where the magical transformation will take place.

Pay REALLY CLOSE ATTENTION to the letter as it burns and FEEL the magic, as before; you can feel the moment when that last connection between the physical paper, envelope and ink is broken and the energy form is released, takes wing and rises away, fast.

It is very, very important that you should feel that; because if you don't, you can't be sure that "something happened, I made something happen" and what happens then is that people look constantly over their shoulder and keep "worrying" about the spell, much like a dog would be worrying their own sore tail, and making worse in the process.

99.9% of all spells cast in good faith, if only they were left to their own devices, would work perfectly well.

It's when people who are unsure if anything happened keep on messing with the ideas and energies after the fact by worrying, repeating the spell unnecessarily, wondering if it will work, and so on and so forth that they destroy the spell, undermine it, essentially worry it to death and nothing good can come of it.

That's like people planting seeds and they keep digging them up again to see if they've sprouted already, if they have a long root now and in the process, destroying the seedlings with their activity.

This is natural to people to do IF THEY DID NOT FEEL THE SPELL WORKING at the time; so make sure you always pay extra close attention to the movements of energy as you are doing any kind of magic so you can know for sure when you did something that rocked the world.

Fire As The Symbol Of Magic

I don't think we can ever know the true impact of awe and astonishment the early human beings felt when someone amongst them first lit a fire.

This is such a profound activity in and of itself that even to this day, delinquents have literal enlightenment experiences when they learn to make a fire by themselves, for the first time, using sticks or flints.

What it was like then, we can't begin to comprehend anymore – it must have been all magic rolled into one and made real for those people at the dawn of humanity.

Even though we have lighters and matches now, and plenty of accelerants, the act of lighting a fire is still connected to that ancient moment of magical awakening, and it is still extremely powerful if we pay attention to it.

It is for this reason that in almost all spiritual and magical traditions, pretty much the very first thing anyone does is to light a fire, a lamp or a candle to commemorate the human spirit awakening.

Single Candle Meditation Exercise

Find a time and place after the sun has set where you can be peaceful and undisturbed.

Take your time and take a while to sit in the darkness; extend your senses into the night and try to connect to what it was like when the nights were really dark indeed, and the moon was the only light source you would find in the night.

Imagine, if you will, what the nights were like back then, and how they had always been until that point, unquestioned, unchanged for these immense time spans that came before.

When you have a sense of this, light the single candle.

Look into the light of the candle, feel its energy with all your senses, this small fire that stands for all fires ever lit by humanity, and allow yourself to be deeply moved by this primal magic.

Make friends with this candle; make friends with the fire; and take this energy and make it your own, make a part of you as a magical human being in the living Universe.

Let this now unfold for you as you will; and when you are ready, blow out the candle with a loving breath but feel the power of heat and fire in your own heart that keeps you warm and safe from within, and connects you to the fire and to your magic, always.

Candle Magic

In this spirit, light candles to announce that magic is about to be happening here again; to start and end ceremonies, spells and rituals; and to remind you always that it is not the material that does the magic, but the magic is in the transfer of energy forms from here to there, and back again.

This basic idea can be used to carry other frequencies across that might be helpful or lifting to your spell; having candles of different colours can shift the vibration of the spell this way, or that.

Of course you can look up "which colours are the right ones" for love spells, money spells and so forth. In the true spirit of energy magic however you should use your own innate knowing, your intuition and also guidance from the powers that be to get you the right colours through FEELING the magic in your body.

So if you have a collection of different coloured candles, and a spell or ritual in mind, you can ask, "Which one is the right one?" and allow yourself to be surprised when the perfect candle for this particular love spell turns out to be the purple one, and not the pink, or red.

Real excellence in magic can ONLY be achieved when you can FEEL which one is the right one; and if you practice that right from the start and take the training wheels of charts and lists of this and that off your magic incarnation, you will get a whole lot further and in much quicker time, at that.

If you remember the transfer exercise with the letter and the fire we talked about earlier, another form of candle magic is to carve symbols or words of intention into a candle which will be transferred slowly to the powers that be as the candle burns down.

As a real magician, you should try all these things for yourself, so you get to experience how they FEEL and what they do, because then you know what they ARE and when the time comes and you need a particular spell, you have experienced these things and you will know right away whether to use for example, a lightning strike transfer of intention from raising energy, put a letter into a fire or burn a candle marked with symbols as the BEST way to achieve THAT particular outcome.

Magic Words

The newest invention amongst people are words.

Much misunderstood, much misused and sadly so often completely disconnected from any form of underlying truth or actual reality, words can be a labyrinth and a hindrance to magic that precludes entrance into the magic realms altogether.

In order to understand words, we have to go back one step and talk about sounds instead.

There are huge amounts of magic in sound; and unfortunately in people, "words" and "music" have become detached from one another.

For magical purposes, both music and words are SOUNDS – vibrations of a particular kind that move the Universe when we create them with our bodies and with our instruments, which came much later.

The Magic Drum

At the heart of the magic of sound and vibration lies the steady beating of a human heart – perhaps the first sound we ever hear in the womb; and a rhythm that is related to all the many rhythms that exist in the Universe and which are the source of the singing all-there-is.

The sound and rhythm of the steady beating of the human heart is the most primal of the drum sounds and the most natural of them all; it takes us back to ourselves and our true natural heritage in a very profound sense, reconnects us to the magical truth of the Universe and moves us away from the every day concerns that flap around our heads most of the time like a herd of marauding crows.

The Magic Drum Exercise

Take a drum or anything that will produce a resonant sound when you strike it with your hand, such as an empty drawer turned upside down, or a wooden bowl.

Find a place of quiet where you can be safe and peaceful; sit down with your drum and breathe deeply.

Relax.

Clear the paths if necessary so you flow smoothly within your emotions, in your mind, in your thinking and you become aware of the sounds around you, and all the feelings in your body.

Keep breathing deeply and focus on the beating of your own heart – FEEL for it in your body, feel for the rhythm.

When you can feel it, gently reach to the drum and begin to tap out that same rhythm.

Get into sync with your heartbeat, and your drum beat.

Remain relaxed and very passive, just noting how that makes you feel, and what energies are beginning to be present there.

Keep it up for as long as you are comfortable, or until you feel you achieved a new understanding.

Sound & Rhythm

There is something very magical about the simple act of "calling a thing by its name". This is the basis of giving a sound to a person or an object or an occurrence, such as saying, "This is Peter," "This is a cup," or "This is the sea."

Before people came to do this strange and magical thing, these kinds of sounds had never been heard on Planet Earth before, and nor had this kind magic taken place.

We modern people think ourselves so smart down the line, but it seems to me that we have lost access to many wonderful and very magical abilities and activities, and have turned them into mundane travesties instead – and definitely, talking and words are high on that list.

To make a connection through which magic and energy may flow, try this following exercise on Spirit Singing (you don't have to be able to "sing" in the common modern sense, nor does it have anything whatsoever to do with singing prettily!).

Spirit Singing Exercise

Find yourself out of doors; if this not physically possible, use the Classic Game to take you to the perfect place in time and space for this exercise.

Find a plant in the environment. Tune into it and give it a spirit name – just a sound, a vibration that you make with your voice. Change your pitch and vibration until you find a match with this one plant – you will feel the CLICK! when that happens.

Now, sing that sound to the plant in a rhythmic pulse. Try faster or slower until you get the click that tells you that you have found the right rhythm for this plant.

You are calling the spirit of the plant by name now and please note how that feels, and how the resonance from the plant responds to that.

After you have had this experience, take some time to reflect upon how you feel about this plant now, what kind of knowing you have about this plant, and what kind of relationship.

If you want to, you can take a drum and call the spirit of the plant with the drum beat alone, or with the drum beat and the spirit song that belongs to that plant.

This is a basic technique that works not just with plants but with rocks, minerals, animals, landscapes, oceans and rivers and with people; it works with angels and entities too, all of which you can call by their spirit name, which isn't just a bunch of letters stuck together but a resonance that has a rhythm, a personal song all of their own.

Power Words & Magic

When we are using words in spells and chants, songs and evocations, prayers and petitions, it is of the essence that the words we use are firstly, absolutely aligned to that which we are trying to achieve (the target) and secondly, that we should evoke these words correctly.

Here is an example.

"She stood by the sea."

You can just read that out aloud and have it mean next to nothing beyond the words themselves.

When we evoke energies with words in spells, we need to evoke the energy behind each one of the words and bring the reality of the existence to life.

In our sentence, that starts with the word, "she".

Who is she?

Look at her, feel her in your body, know her and let her energy flow through you, build up and become evoked and manifest when you say the word, "she" and it literally flows with your breath from your mouth and stands in the room as an energetic reality (that by the way, other people then can also touch if they pay attention).

Take the next word - "stood". She didn't dance, or lie down, or slouch, or crawl around, or walk or run – she STOOD.

There is a particular energy occurrence here, a particular

kind of movement that is straight and holding position with volition. Know what that feels like to "stand" and only when you can feel that, give voice to it and say the word, "stood".

"By the" and "sea" are the shore, and the water respectively.

Both are truly amazing occurrences in their own right; know, feel, understand the shore, connect to the shore, and then the sea just the same.

Now you are ready to speak your first magic sentence as you raise all these energies in turn and make them manifest -

"She stood by the sea."

How does that make you feel?

Does that give you a little inkling of the power of words, if they are used in a magical way?

Please know that with so many things, this gets even better with age, wisdom and experience.

Words, if you use them like that, will never be the same again, and if you want to, you can speak with power at any time you choose to do so. I do not just mean that you can speak spells with great power, but also words that you use in every day such as, "Put the gun down," or "Give me the best price," or "You are beautiful," for example.

Words always have the potential to be magical and once we know this, we can pick up on this power at any time.

Rhyming Spells

In our earlier example, "She stood by the sea," there is actually a rhythm in that one short, single sentence. It didn't rhyme because there wasn't a second line, but you can feel the flow of that single sentence well enough if you pay attention.

When we create a spell, a chant, something for a ritual and so forth that we want to be magically resonant, it becomes very natural to make it have a rhythm, and a rhyme that pulses the sounds and makes the energy forms cohesive so they survive the transfer from us into the all-there-is intact enough so that the metaphorical letter we are sending to the powers that be arrives complete and not in unreadable tatters.

As always, clear your mind of any and all nonsense you have ever heard about poetry, rhyming, and any ideas you might have about your talents in the Shakespeare department; what we do when we write or create a rhyming spell has, as usual nothing to do with any of that.

The English language is fabulous for rhyming because there are so many words that end on the same sounds; it is really easy to find a rhyme on just about everything if you take heed not to put words such as orange, ultraviolet or purple at the end of a line ☺

Rather than sitting with paper and pen and "trying to

construct a spell that rhymes" with furrowed brow, speaking with rhyme and rhythm is a learned skill that starts to FLOW with a little practice.

I once wrote this fun instruction:

A Little Rhyming Spell For Witches

Why don't you just speak in rhyme
for a day, and all the time?
Sister, brother, mother mild,
you can drive them screaming wild,
when they ask you for advice
and you rhyme your answer thrice
Every sentence that you speak
you must rhyme and rhythm seek
and what happens after time
is your brain will do this fine
doesn't have to be so good
long as you are understood
its a simple skill you see
you can learn that - one, two three!
When the time comes then your way
where a spell you have to say
it will come in rhyming form
it is easily the norm!
words will flow with elegance
lead their own amazing dance

rhyming isn't hard you see
lots of words from a to z
you can play with anytime
that is how you learn to rhyme!

If you can't match this up in your mind with deeply meaningful and complex "dead serious rituals," let me remind you that we said that magic is light hearted and joyous in essence, and yes, you can have fun with the practice of magic!

- **Energy is light and if it flows brightly, it sparkles and zings, makes you feel alive, makes you feel YOUNG.**

So this is a good time to be learning and re-affirming these important lessons of magic, to be light of heart, clap your hands, find your rhythm and simply have a go at speaking some words with the intention that they will rhyme and pulse.

Like practising scales on the piano with the idea that your fingers learn where to find the sounds again so that if you want to get to a particular sound, you can reach it quickly and without thinking about it, practising fun rhyming in different rhythmic lengths and beat speeds will train you into the skill to find the right words at the right moment.

This is particularly important to do "magic of the moment" most beautifully; but also for any other form of spell, chant, incantation, ritual, evocation or even to address the powers that be, to be able to flow these expressions from the heart, in the moment, spontaneously and uniquely for each occasion, this is a wonderful skill and help to make your magic come alive.

I would like to note that this skill applied to other things, that are normally not considered to be high magic, such as writing a love poem that will turn an intended's heart and make them yours forever, or a bereavement note that will have the power to soothe the raw pain of the recipient, or an advertisement that will cause to put the prospects to put their hands in their purses, can also be considered to be an application of magic, if you want it to be so.

In working with magic wordcraft, the evocation of the actual reality behind the words, the rhythm and flow of the energetic unfoldment and the resonance effects this produces on reality itself, we have a gift of tremendous proportions that is ours from the moment we learn to speak – if only we knew that and recognised it.

I am quite delighted that this human talent is being revived in the new interest in modern magic; and I have some hope that there will be more people as a result who will have the power to look to someone's eyes, say, "I love you," and have that be real, and so that you can feel it.

Love Poem Exercise

Where does a love spell start and a love poem end?

I think if they are good, they are indistinguishable from one another and in fact, are one and the same.

Bearing in mind what we have learned about rhythm, rhyme, evoking energetic realities and speaking with the heart, now create a love poem for someone you truly love.

Think about what we said about the archer, and that you really have to FEEL the magic when you deliver the final result as you would cast a spell, in this case by speaking the poem out aloud, or evoking it, if you will.

You can make this as long or as short as you want it to be; and do the best you can, with a pure heart.

Allow yourself to be surprised at what you have already learned, what you can do, and how this kind of magic can make you feel.

The Magic Machine

With the 23 Genius Symbols, we have an alphabet of energy forms that we can use to create, shape and change energetic realities.

You can use the symbols together with the usual kinds of spell ingredients or by themselves to create powerful spells, charms, magical objects and rituals of transformation.

As there are no negatively charged symbols in the set, they do not attract unwanted visitors or energy forms; indeed, the symbols are unpalatable and unattractive to the kind of astral pests that have plagued magicians since the dawn of time and will act to keep them away.

At the same time, because of the love and lightness in the symbols, helpful spirits and entities are attracted to the symbols and especially to the symbol sphere. That is extremely radiant in and of itself.

The symbols replace a wide variety of different types of signs, sigils and so forth and because they are easy to understand, they are easy and rewarding to work with, plus they will give you RELIABLE results, even in the hands of a beginner.

No Reversed Symbols

I would like to mention that the symbols cannot be "reversed" meaning that when you use them for divination or fortune telling, or in any other way, you can't turn them "evil" by turning them upside down.

The energy forms are set and they are what they are, no matter which way up they land, or which way you turn them.

Further, the symbols aren't flat, even if they are represented on flat stones or a piece of card.

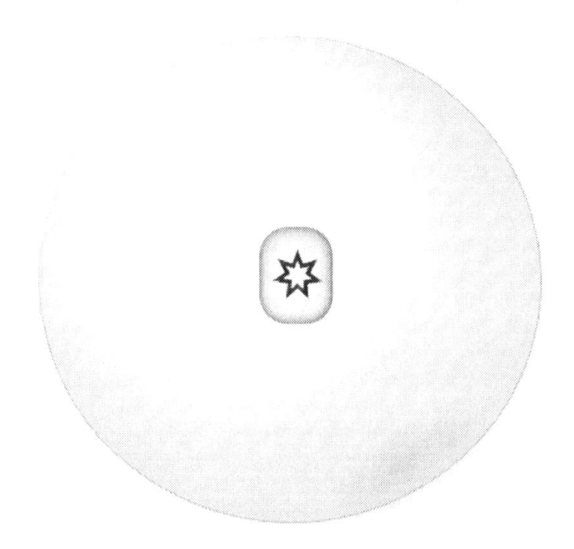

Each symbol is a sphere in its own right and radiates out into all directions and all dimensions.

The Basic Symbol Sphere

When you sit down at a table, or on the floor, and arrange the symbols in a circle, you are creating your own personal Stonehenge type of magic circle; only you retain the overview over the entire magic sphere as you look down from above, and so you can steer not just what goes on inside the circle, but also what happens to the entire sphere that contains the spell.

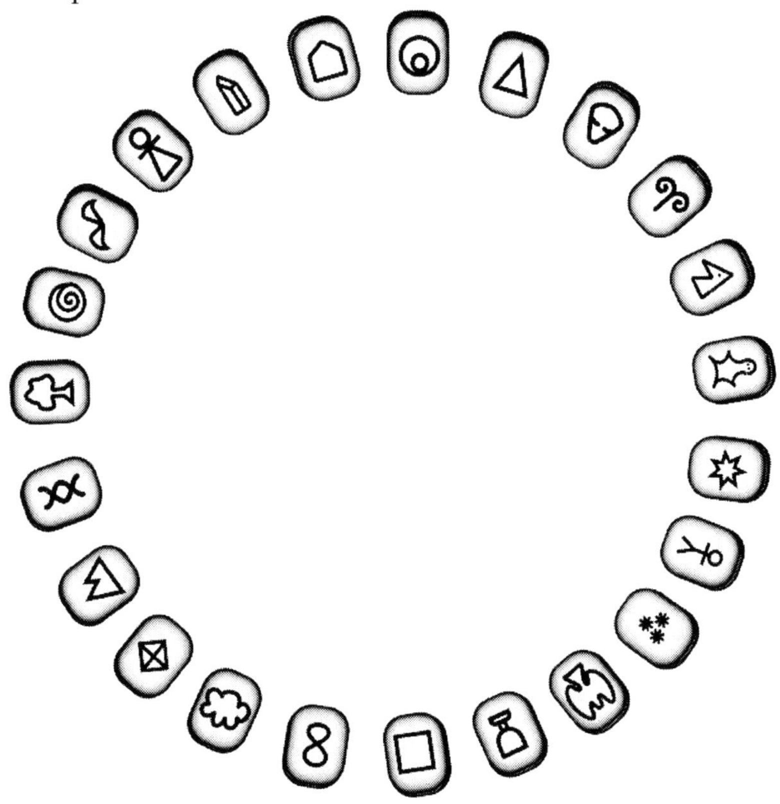

You might have noticed by now that the symbols are NOT numbered. Not only that, every time we have seen them so far they were in a different order.

- **That is because these symbols are NOT number based, do NOT have a hierarchy, and do NOT march in straight lines according to rank.**

These symbols are a little too complex for that!

When you create a basic symbol sphere, and that means no more and no less than taking your symbols out and arranging them in a circle, you are already making use of the amazing flexibility of how these symbols interact with you and with each other.

There are 23x23 different ways in which a symbol sphere can be arranged just by placement, and you can times that by 360 or infinity if you get more fluent still with how you place each symbol.

I am just telling you this to have you **get a feel for the FLUIDITY of a symbol sphere**.

It is not always the same.

Sometimes it can be larger, sometimes it is smaller; and where the individual symbols take their place within the circle depends on where you put them on that day.

So how do you know where the symbols go?

The answer to that is that you CANNOT KNOW – until you've decided first what it is that you are going to do.

- **Whatever it is that you are going to do is going to be supported by the construction of a sphere FOR THAT PURPOSE as you place the markers that contain the symbols, one at a time.**

So hold your intention on the target by saying out aloud and saying in your mind at the same time in chorus,

"Dear symbols, today we are going to create a powerful protection charm for Mike who is about to go to war with the fellow soldiers in his regiment."

... and then place the symbols as it feels right to you.

If you have any sense, intuition or magic feelers AT ALL, you will already begin to feel the power build up in the sphere from this moment forward.

As you are building up the power AND THE INTENTION of the sphere, it begins to "burn more brightly" and can now be seen and noticed by the powers that be who are always on the lookout for a light that shines in the darkness.

They are attracted by this, and as this sphere has already a very specific vibration, which in this case INCLUDES MIKE, another person who ALSO has guardian angels and spirits that would help him, even if he doesn't know this at all, with a set up such as this you can expect that not only the powers that be that usually work with you will be in attendance, but also other helpful spirits.

You don't have to ask them to attend, they are drawn naturally to what you are doing.

That is a really extraordinary effect of using the symbols as a "magic machine" and for you as the person who is facilitating and guiding this, it's an extraordinary experience as you became aware of not just your friends entering the vicinity and lending their strength and blessing to this endeavour, but also as these strangers come, Mike's crew, if you will, and these are often beings that you would otherwise have never met.

I have done this a few times and I can tell you that once you've worked with someone else's crew as well, a relationship comes into being with those guys; I don't know if we can say that they are grateful and/or delighted that you are helping their man in this way, but I certainly have the feeling that if you ever needed their help in the future for something, they too would be available to you, even if it wasn't about their man at all at that time.

I also believe strongly that these helpful spirits that each person has, whether they know it or not, are really happy when they are called upon to be with us.

I get the sense that they WANT to help us out and will literally JUMP at an opportunity offered to lend their aid. Which makes me think about why it is that even we don't ask for help enough, don't allow them to do more for us.

Working the symbol spheres gives them more access to us as well, and I have had numerous experiences where they were able to use that access from their end and send me important information WITHOUT me having to open the portal. I think that is really important, because when you are sick, or in danger, or freaked out, that they can reach out to you, without you having to do all the work, is pretty priceless.

- **To sum up: When we make a symbol sphere, the individual symbols form a unique sphere every time. That is the baseline of the spell. As a side effect, the strong radiation from the sphere attracts helpful entities, just as it repels unhelpful ones.**

From the moment you start with the symbols, you are therefore guided, empowered AND protected in your magic work – and that is very important for us beginners, as we all are, in these realms of magic.

The Centre Of The Sphere

The centre of the sphere is the focal point for the spell; it is there that you set the specific intention, the target, and that is where the focus of power for all the symbols lies.

The symbol sphere is so incredibly versatile and useful because you can place absolutely anything at all into the centre of the sphere.

In this example, a photograph of a person is in the central position.

But you can have anything at all there.

You can have a piece of paper with a person's name on it.

You can have a piece of paper with a request on it.

You can place a glass of water in the centre that you wish to turn into a magic potion.

You can place an already made magic potion that has a number of different ingredients in the focus and kick the energetic effectiveness of that potion up to the hilt by charging it so.

You can place any object, any artefact into the centre or the sphere and act upon it, transfer it, change it.

If the object doesn't fit into the centre, let's say you wanted to put safety and blessing on a person's car, you can use a representation of the car, the number plate on a piece of paper, or you can take the symbols out and place them around the actual physical object.

That is perfectly doable, and there might be times when you want to do just that.

I would like to note that you can use a symbol sphere also to clean objects that have been purposefully or accidentally imprinted, such as a second hand ring, or a crystal that had picked up some disturbing vibrations along the way, or a charm you made yourself for a particular purpose and now you want to use that piece of jewellery again for something else because you like wearing it.

Setting the intention for the symbols sphere that you make on this occasion to act as a powerful energy washing machine and freshner/brightner for such an object will make it good as new and rearing to go with something else again.

The Speed Of Magic

Now is probably a good time to mention that we must beware of getting snared in hard thinking about how long it takes for a spell to work.

Planting a seed for example takes AGES to show any results in the hard, and even when they finally do, we're dealing with two teensy leaves that are no good to anyone yet until some ten, twenty summers have passed and finally you get a good crop of cherries.

Magic isn't at all anything like that.

It's magic, right?

Pull up the spiral and remember...

You can clean a ring that was worn by someone day in, day out, for 65 years in an INSTANCE – flash, caboom, DONE.

You don't have to "soak" spells overnight like trying to get blood out of a linen shirt or softening up dried lentils; magic is FAST.

It's so fast, fast is no longer the word for it!

The speed at which any spell works is actually set ENTIRELY, and I mean ENTIRELY, by the human practitioner who is performing this.

Let's face it – either it worked or it didn't; either the powers that be got it, or they didn't, and another week on the remedial bench isn't going to do the trick.

Start questioning yourself when you get into this idea that any spell must sit there in the symbol sphere for a day, or a week, or even an hour for it to work.

This is not the case. Remember that magic is a FLASH that changes the Universe; and even if you take your time getting there, eventually there has to be a FLASH.

So you might as well save yourself a lot of time and work towards the FLASH as fast as you can; our hours in physical form are indeed, limited and we should try and make the most of it.

When you get a strong idea that the symbol sphere you made "needs to stay like that for a week" I would recommend going inside and checking out what's going on, why you think you (or the recipient) need this extra time before they (become fully protected, get rich, heal, get on with their love affair, find a new house, etc. ad infinitum).

It might be a good idea to run the "clearing the paths" over this issue or topic a few more times so you can go forward now – and fast, allowing magic to do it's thing, and that takes no time at all.

Powering Up The Sphere

The most powerful and complete version of the symbol sphere is to power up every single symbol, one at a time, for that specific purpose of the spell.

We had, as an example, Mike who is about to go to war, and a protection charm is being made for him that he will wear to keep out of harms way and to be magically protected from all manner of danger.

We have put out the symbols already with that in mind, and you can already feel that presences are with us now who are supporting us in this endeavour – our spirit crew, and also likely Mike's crew, as well.

Now, we add the blessing of each symbol, each energy form by touching the symbol and drawing a line with our finger, or a magic wand if you prefer to be slightly more theatrical, and EVOKE each symbol for this purpose fully:

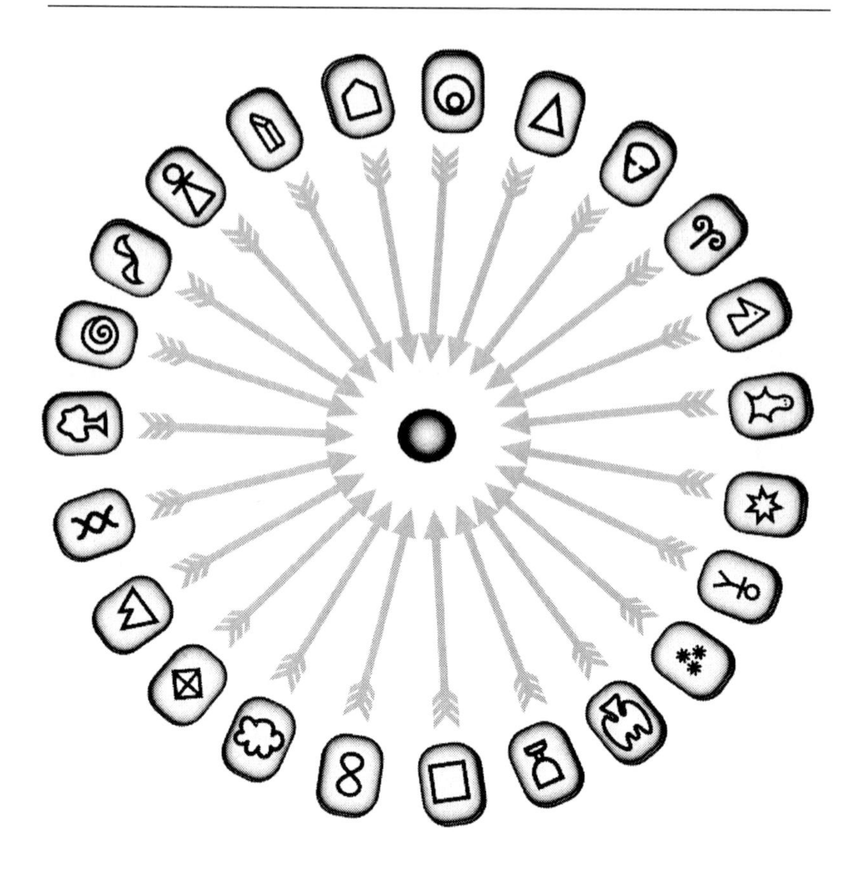

- I charge you to protect Mike in all his trades and exchanges.
- *I charge you to protect Mike and all his aspects for his highest good.*
- *I charge you to protect Mike from alien influences.*
- *I charge you to protect Mike with the power of creativity.*
- *I charge you to protect Mike with the power of the animal kingdom.*
- *I charge you to protect Mike with the power of the spirit kingdom.*
- *I charge you to protect Mike in the name of the light.*

- *I charge you to protect Mike through, and from other people.*
- *I charge you to protect Mike with the power of the realm of pure potential.*
- *I charge you to protect Mike with the power of the angels.*
- *I charge you to protect Mike with and from the world of man made things.*
- *I charge you to protect Mike in space.*
- *I charge you to protect Mike in time.*
- *I charge you to protect Mike and his emotions.*
- *I charge you to protect Mike with miraculous gifts and in miraculous ways.*
- *I charge you to protect Mike with the power of the land.*
- *I charge you to protect Mike through the power of the dance.*
- *I charge you to protect Mike through the power of the plant kingdom.*
- *I charge you to protect Mike and his spirit for his highest good.*
- *I charge you to protect Mike through hearing and paying attention to his friends.*
- *I charge you to protect Mike with logic and clarity.*
- *I charge you to protect Mike and the houses he dwells in.*

As you can notice, there is no real "formula" to how I interpreted the protection that is available through each symbol on this occasion.

For this example, I tuned into each symbol and asked

what it had to give, specifically, to strengthen the spell and the charm that will be result of the spell.

When you do this yourself, you can feel the power building up and up, as you add one energy form after the other and they all start to resonate together, COME TOGETHER in that original "I charge you to protect Mike," which is the core, the centre, the heart and the true target of the spell.

Casting The Spell

By now, the symbol sphere is vibrating on your table and you should really feel that energy build up in your whole body. I personally stand up for this next part, I find it simply more comfortable and conducive to that energy flow.

Hold your hands over the sphere and unite it all now in that one final energy discharge into the charm as you direct all that built up power down and into the charm in the centre of the sphere:

I charge you to protect Mike.

Let all the power from you, from the symbols, and from the helpers present RUSH into that charm as one, fast.

That should be a really noticeable experience that leaves you high and in a "wow!" state, tingling with the aftershocks of this energy – and in the centre of your symbol sphere, there lies a charm that is so radiant with power, it's nearly hopping off the table.
I like to pick this object up, seal it with a kiss, thank the powers that be and also the symbols that are now lying quietly and relaxed and are waiting to be put back into their normal resting place.
Well done!

THE SILENT SYMBOL SPHERE

Now the full symbol sphere is a powerful piece of magic indeed; but there might be times when a slightly different approach is required.

I have found a wonderfully soothing energy support structure is being created when you use a silent symbol sphere – this is all the symbols, but turned face down.

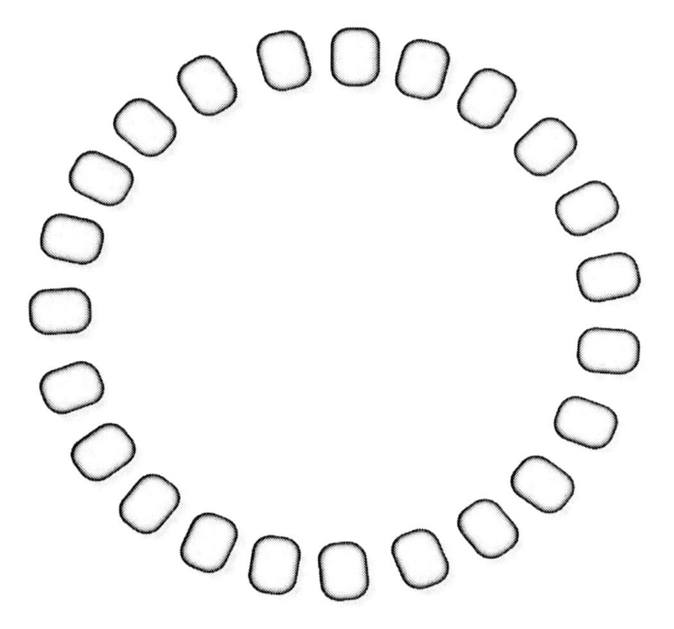

They are still broadcasting their energies, but they are working together without your conscious guidance; the fact that you "can't see" the symbols drawn upon the markers is a metaphorical withdrawal of your conscious steering, and putting the symbol sphere on autopilot so it can do it's own thing, and send energies of support through time, space and the dimensions.

As with the active symbol sphere, you place the

markers in accordance to the target that needs this "silent support" but you place them face down and let the energy build up that way. Then you place your directional device (photo, charm, words written on paper) in the centre and let the symbol sphere rise up and do its own thing from that moment forth.

There is no energy input from you required and in the case of the silent symbol sphere, you end up very relaxed and dreamy rather than highly charged and with electricity sparking from your finger tips.

Silent symbol spheres are very magical and you will know when you need one of those – you will feel it with your magic spider sense. ☺

Choosing Specific Vibrations

Much as I love the entire sphere, with all elements working together, I personally find using not all but some of the symbols to create a specific outcome particularly delightful.

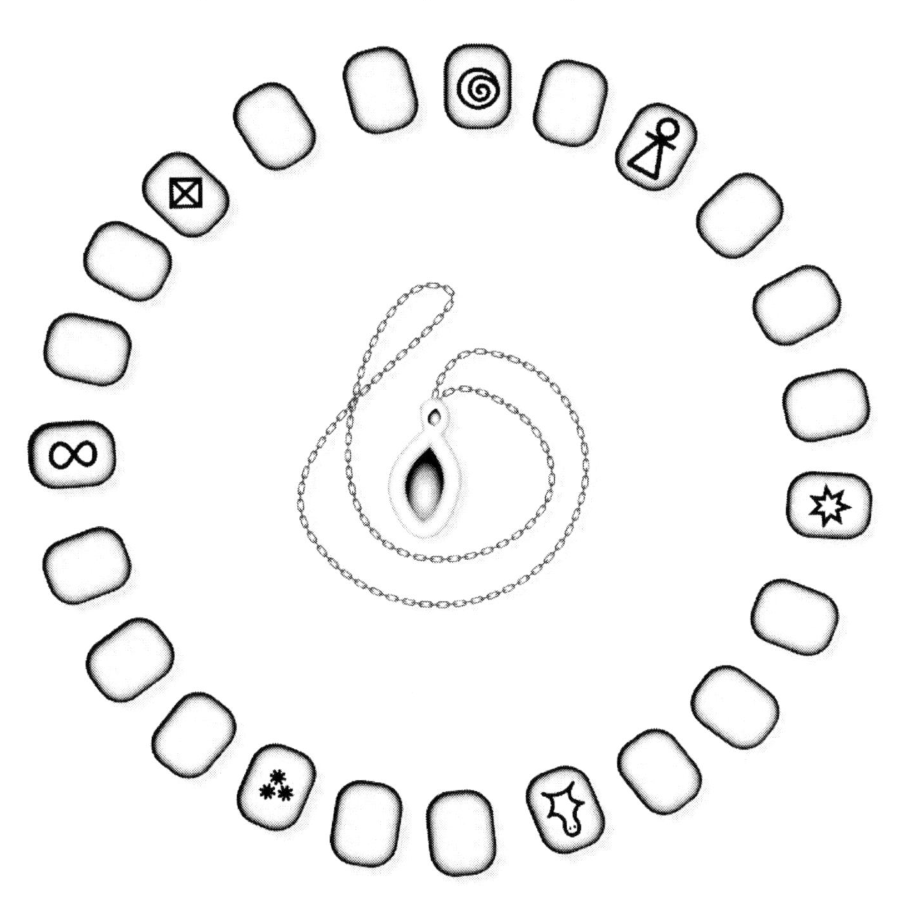

In this example, only some of the symbols are active to charge the pendant in the centre of the sphere; the rest are present and lend their silent support.

A little exercise: See if you can figure out or get a sense of what this pendant is going to be used for.

FEEL for the energy forms which are being directed at the pendant, and get a feel for this symbols sphere where those particular seven symbols are active, and the rest give silent support.

Another little exercise: Imagine you were making a prosperity pendant for a particular friend (not for yourself!).

Which symbols would you have active on this occasion, and which would lend their silent support?

The Focused Symbol Charging

We can align the energy forms in the focus centre of the sphere by creating a magic circle of silent support and bringing the energy forms we want to use to charge the object or create the spell in closer.

That looks like this:

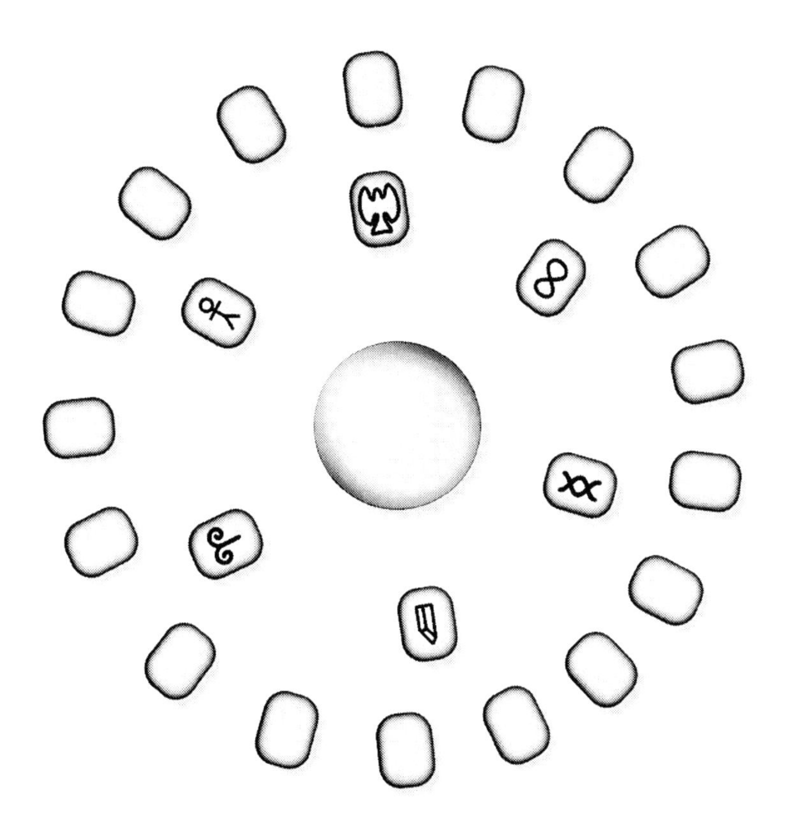

What happens here energetically is that the outer silent circle focuses their energy THROUGH the symbols in the inner circle and thus lends this configuration "extra punch".

In this case, a crystal ball is being charged for a very particular session where these exact energy forms are required.

Magic Perfume Exercise

As an exercise that is good fun and to get an experience of this extra focus punch effect, try the following.

Use a bottle of perfume or aftershave and decide what type of magic potion you want to add to what already exists in the bottle as it is.

You might want to add some magic, or fairy dust, or perhaps a little light to "increase your X factor" when you spray that perfume or aftershave onto your person.

Give it a good shot, remember the archer, let the energy build up and let it FLASH into the focus point, which would be the perfume bottle at the centre of the symbol sphere.

Pay attention to how people respond differently to you, depending on what you do with this potion, and also remember that you can clear it all out again and try something else if the results were not quite what you had expected at your first attempt. ☺

The Symbol Wave

There are many different ways in which you can choose the symbols that make up a potion, a charm or a spell.

You can use a pendulum in the symbol sphere; your can let your magic feeling guide you to right one. You can pick a "random" selection of symbols from the deck, or you can take a journey to help you discover what you need to add to make a complete spell/potion for this particular purpose.

A nice way to practice a number of magical skills at the same time as finding the right ingredients for your spell is the symbol wave.

Place the symbols face down (for a beginner) and face up (for a more aware practitioner of magic) in a wave form like this:

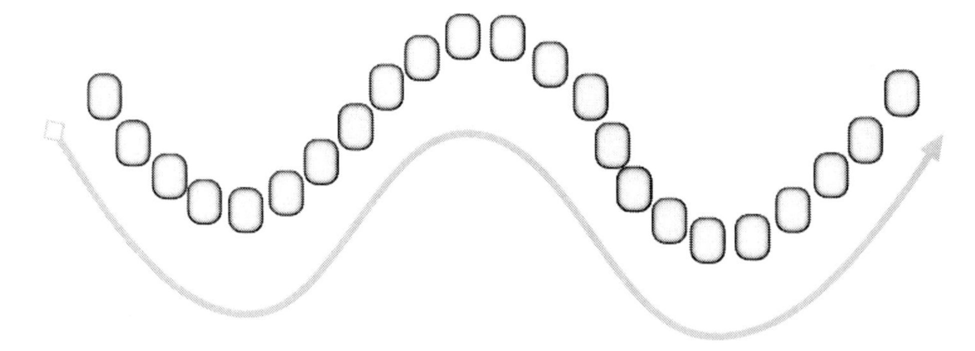

State the purpose of the spell or potion, for example:

"I want to make a healing potion for Aunt Sheryl."

Gently run your hand (I like to use the back of my hand as that is extra sensitive) in a wave form over the symbol wave and stop when you FEEL that one of the symbols stands out energetically.

Take that symbol out and move it down; this is the first component for your symbol cocktail.

Now repeat until all the correct components have been extracted; now you can turn them over and see what your spell will contain.

You can inscribe these symbols on objects, with paint or with a wand; use them in a focused sphere to charge potions, charms, objects and send healing, protection or change spell to people, objects, systems and situations.

You can also use these symbols to make symbol sigils for special purposes.

Symbol Sigils

People like to make geometrical objects and mandalas; symbol sigils can be used to seal intentions onto objects and they will keep working as they are going "around and around" and keep channelling energy through themselves for as long as they remain in existence.

Designs created from, or containing symbols can be used around the house, to decorate furniture and all manner of objects, clothes, note books and whatever else you want to imbue with extra magic power according to your needs.

Here are some examples:

Success Sigil For An Artist

If you notice this symbol starts with The Gift – the miracle, the surprise, that which you didn't do anything to deserve. There is creativity and genesis, interestingly aspects which may describe aspects of the artist but also, different aspects of art; this artist wants to work in more than just one medium.

The outer symbols are time, and trade – the works of art will stand the test of time and grow over time, become blessed by time itself, and they are going to make money in exchange for that original gift they bring to those who own them.

Please note: Although you can, of course, copy this

sigil, it is MUCH MORE BENEFICIAL to make your own, or have someone make one personally for one particular artist. This one was made for one very special artist and their path; I do believe all artists are special, and should have their own custom made sigil!

Magic Circle Sigil

This simple, straightforward and powerful sigil was used by a "magic circle of friends," ten people who wanted to unite in magic, do magic together and express this through the people in the circle. All wore this sigil in various ways and used it to invoke the power of the group, not just their own friends, but everyone's helpers in a "one for all, and all for one" attitude.

The simplicity and directness of this sigil is probably one of its best assets and greatest power.

Sigil For Soul Protection

Here, "the magic within" is protected by higher forces and by the light.

Simple and effective.

This sigil was made for a child in difficult circumstances.

Protection Sigil For A House

This is a particular protection device made for a particular house in which a particular family lived under (yes, that's right!) unique and particular circumstances.

As an exercise try to read this sigil backwards so you can de-code what the circumstances might be that would cause THIS sigil to come into being, and not all the other infinite possibilities of combinations of symbols to form a circle.

This is also a really good example of the merit of making a sigil for each individual case, so it really fits and can do the job precisely, quickly, and powerfully well.

A Sigil For ...?

This last one I'm going to leave for you to read and work out what that is, and what that does.

Don't try and think about it too much, touch it instead, FEEL IT, and let the information come to you in that special magical way as energy flows into you, through and out.

If all else should fail, take a short journey and find out that way what this sigil was made for, and what it does.

Sigils are good fun to make, and with the symbols being easy to draw and having a multitude of geometrical possibilities, you can make all manner of patterns and tapestries you can use in so many different ways in your life and in your magic work.

Fortune Telling With The Genius Symbols

Fortune telling relies on being able to "see the future" and the symbols make it easy to open up streams of visions, directed by the set up in use for fortune telling.

There are two parts to fortune telling therefore – seeing the vision, and then interpreting it so that the querent gets something beneficial out of it.

This is where fortune telling crosses over with dream interpretation in traditional magic as it is the same skill to interpret a vision correctly as it is to interpret a dream.

As we have already noted, a proper vision is not just seeing things, but also hearing, touching and most importantly, FEELING what goes on so we get the full information content.

Visions also need to be alive, that means they are moving like real life would, they are not just a still photograph of a single scene with the soundtrack turned off.

If you are an absolute beginner, you will experience what we call flash visions as you tune in and out randomly of probably more than one TV channel, for the want of a better metaphor. So you get quick impressions of a face here, a bunch of cowboys chasing Indians there, a ship here and some people cooking over there as you're skipping through the channels.

This can be confusing, as you can imagine ☺ but by keeping your stress down, clearing the paths and letting the symbols help you, you can find that visions stand steady and resonantly and you can understand the information – if you let the movie play for long enough.

That's the next place at which beginners make a mistake in fortune telling – they shut off the information too soon. Sure, there's a tall and dark stranger, but so what? What happens next? The whole point about fortune telling is to foresee the future so that the right action in the HERE AND NOW may be taken to avoid danger and move towards pleasure and success.

The final place where beginners go wrong with fortune telling is that they try to tell their own fortune exclusively. Telling your own fortune is like drilling and filling your own teeth – it's really difficult and not many people would even try, especially those who know something about dentistry.

Even with path clearing and a whole lot of self knowledge, there is just too much going on for too many reasons to be able to take a good overview of one's own future; and for a beginner, it is near enough impossible.

So in order to practice fortune telling successfully, you **MUST READ FOR OTHERS**.

Magic As A Social Activity

Here is a good time now to mention that magic is in essence a highly social activity. In the primal days of human evolution, there was but one shaman for a whole tribe, doing all the magic for everyone and on everyone's behalf.

These guys were doing a lot of magic, every day; and so it is no wonder they got good at it over a few decades.

As a "single practitioner" or "solitary witch" (and my, doesn't that sound sad!) you are not going to get the practice the old shaman used to get – until you understand that magic is a very social activity, requires a lot of social skills, and the practice you need to get good at it comes through relationships with other people, other things and other beings.

I was highly amused to note as I thought about this that being competent with others and having good social skills is actually a strong pre-requisite for being a good magician.

It is not so much being able to communicate with people successfully, but really the communication skills required to deal with entities and spirits well; with animals, making relationships that work with symbols and with plants, with landscapes. All of that is communication skills, social skills which makes a practitioner of magic in the end someone who has

MORE relationships, deeper relationships and with a much, much wider divergence of beings and existences than someone who parties all day and night and spends their lives surrounded by dozens of family members and friends.

Often, people who are drawn to magic specifically DON'T want to get involved with relationships, especially with people; they see magic as an escape from other people and a protection from intimate relationships.

That is fine because the practice of real magic does reconnect a person to others outside of them, and it heals them and their relationships eventually, if they keep going long enough.

If you keep going long enough with magic, you will make relationships that work.

Perhaps at first with something as non-threatening and far away from a human as you can get, such as a crystal – being touched by its pureness and beauty and wanting to love it and receive its energies in return. Some people start by loving the land, some by loving animals, some by loving plants and herb lore; some by loving spirits and angels and fairies.

All of that is a starting point, a "way in" to or back into that whole relationship thing which will eventually once more involve – people.

The fact is that there are only so many spells you can cast on your own behalf before you run out of ideas. There is only one future of your own you can query and to do that time and time again is just – weird, and can't lead to any good. There are only so many charms you can hang around your own neck, and only so many potions you can take every day. Exceed that, and all you do is cause chaos in your own incarnation – and many witches do precisely that.

An OUTLET is needed for using magic energy, and having magic energy experiences, and one person simply isn't enough of an outlet.

To be a really good magician and to understand magic, understand your own talents and skills, how they work, and most of all to EVOLVE as a magical person you need to USE MAGIC – a lot.

Some people take this understanding and become professional witches and psychics and so find an outlet for their magic activities that way; but for most people that's not an option and so we have to think creatively to provide ourselves with the practice we need so we can get better at magic and fulfil that basic social contract of magic that drives the usage of a magician's skill towards using it on behalf of other people.

The easiest and safest way to do this is to take querents in Sanctuary.

- **As we go through the fortune telling patterns and exercises, I would like you to practice these things by using the Classic Game to "take you to the perfect place in time and space where I can meet the right querents to help me learn and practice my fortune telling".**

In Sanctuary, you will have a literally never ending stream of querents who will ask you all sorts of questions, and these will have been "brought to you" specially selected to be a good match with you and your skills at this time. Further, each client/querent you read for and work with in Sanctuary will be teaching YOU something important as well; this of course is the same for living querents, should you have those as well.

By using Sanctuary querents to ask you for spells, to make charms, and to tell fortunes ON THEIR BEHALF, your own magic skills and powers can begin to FLOW and flower safely. You never need make a move to living clients and querents and stay physically solitary that way, but you will get all the benefits an experienced shaman would be getting from being asked to perform many tasks and do many different things on behalf of a wide variety of querents.

This is a great example of how "being selfish" only works when you are being intelligently selfish and engage in the service of others; because those who don't get stuck on their two or three attempts at doing this, or that, and that is all they will ever know, and never get good at magic in the process.

- **In short: To learn to do good fortune telling, DO IT FOR OTHERS. That way you keep a clear head, a good overview, and become a better fortune teller.**

A Simple Single Symbol Reading Example

All the symbols are portals to entire worlds; they are also portals to entire visions.

The symbols are also universal, meaning that people can know them and have a resonance to them, even if they haven't been told what the symbols mean or what they stand for.

This being so, you can use a single symbol chosen by the querent themselves to start a flow of vision that will be beneficial and gratefully accepted by the querent, and found to be useful.

I'm now going to give an example of using a Sanctuary reading with three Sanctuary querents and the simple single symbol set up.

"Take me to the perfect place in time and space where I can meet querents to practice my single symbol readings."

It is mid morning, spring, the weather is alright, a little breezy, and I am in a tent that has been pitched under an old lime tree. It's open at the front and this is clearly a festival, with many people walking by and I can hear music and smell something like donuts. At the back of the tent on a cushion sleeps my familiar, a stray dog that came to me one day. He "has my back" which I appreciate when I drift off and out into visions in public and makes sure no-one runs off with the till.

I have the symbols face up on pretty sparkling multi-coloured glass cabochons; they flash in the light and attract people's attention. I see that I have put up a sign that offers a single symbol reading for a single coin.

The first person to approach is an old man who is half dragging his wife behind. She is clearly not into spending money with a fortune teller, but he is very keen and ignores her.

He hands me the coin and I direct him to pick one of the symbols.

He picks the Weather symbol, the little cloud.

As I look at the symbol I get a sense of thunder and lightning, lightning strike – I say to the man that he gets pain striking him when the weather changes and he is amazed because that is spot on. It is making his life a misery and he can't sleep; in the day he is waiting for this pain to strike randomly. I ask him if he has seen a doctor and he says no, he doesn't believe in doctors. I tell him that this pain is the bane of his life and he has to deal with it, do something about it, this is my message for him today. The man nods thoughtfully, sighs, thanks me and walks away with his wife.

The second querent is already waiting, a young girl. She hands over her coin and picks the alien symbol. I look at it and smile and say, "Are you in love with an alien?" She looks wide eyed in surprise, blushes deeply and then says yes, she is in love with someone she doesn't understand at all. I tell her that there is nothing wrong with loving an alien but you have to not expect them to be like normal people, make allowances, and make an effort to learn more about them and their ways, not judge them up front, and then things can work out fine. She is delighted and thanks me many times before skipping away with a song in her step.

The final person on this occasion is a pale young man. I have spotted him loitering around, trying to pick up his courage. He very much wants a reading but he is scared and very nervous, torn between needing magic help and not believing in magic and cursing himself for a fool for wanting it in his life.

Eventually, he comes over, doesn't look me in the eye and slides the coin on the table top towards the till. I tell him to choose a symbol. He asks how he is supposed to do that, shouldn't I choose one for him? "I can if you want," I say, "but I think as it's your life, it should be your symbol. Just pick one."

He dithers and hesitates, but I notice his eyes keep coming back and back to the Crystal symbol. Eventually I say to him, "You keep looking at this one, shall we say this is it?" He is very relieved and nods rapidly.

I pick up the crystal symbol and hold it in my hand. The cool clarity of that symbol is like the antidote to all his confused emanations that are making me quite tired, and I'm only watching him from the outside, and only for such a short time. I can't imagine what it must be like to live like that, all the time. No wonder he looks so pained, pale and skinny.

I say to him, "You need clarity and logic, something to hold on to, and if there is an opportunity for you do get involved in something that is very clear and logical, you should do so because that will give you Sanctuary, will give you time to grow stronger."

He nods as I speak, very rapidly, and some colour is flushing in his cheeks. He says in a rush, "I was thinking about studying science but I wasn't sure if I was smart enough."

I say, "The symbol says you need the logic." He says, "I do, it's true." He sighs and feels much calmer now and there is even a smile for me as he thanks me and walks away.

And there, we have it.☺

Three querents, three single symbol readings.

It didn't take very long to do, and I now have three extra experiences that I didn't have before.

I also have three coins, a dog spirit I didn't know before and a new world discovered, a new place I can visit again and use for future practice of my magic skills.

Most of all, I have the MEMORY of these three readings; and should it ever come to pass that I am called upon to do this in the hard, I'll be doing it AGAIN and not for the first time.

Working magic in Sanctuary, using the Classic Game to get you to the "perfect place in time and space" cannot be recommended highly enough, nor can it be appreciated highly enough as an opportunity to step into whole new realms of finding out who you are, and what you can REALLY accomplish by and with magic.

The Three Symbol Reading

This is a simple past, present and future pattern from left to right.

Again, do try and avoid doing these for yourself, and especially more than once; you are going to confuse yourself and lose the plot.

When you practice these, call to mind a querent and do it for them instead.

You don't have to do the whole Classic Game journey experience I showed you earlier; simply imagine that a friend or someone you like, a movie star or a TV presenter, or anyone at all is sitting next to you and you are doing this reading for THEM.

By the way, don't get distraught if your imaginary querent gets upset or says your reading wasn't any good. In fact, I should celebrate that as a clear cut piece of evidence that you are definitely not "making it all up" and you are learning something that is quite real here!

Should that come to pass, ask a guide to come and negotiate peace, explain what went wrong so that all concerned can learn something from it, and leave happily from this astral session.

The Zodiac Reading

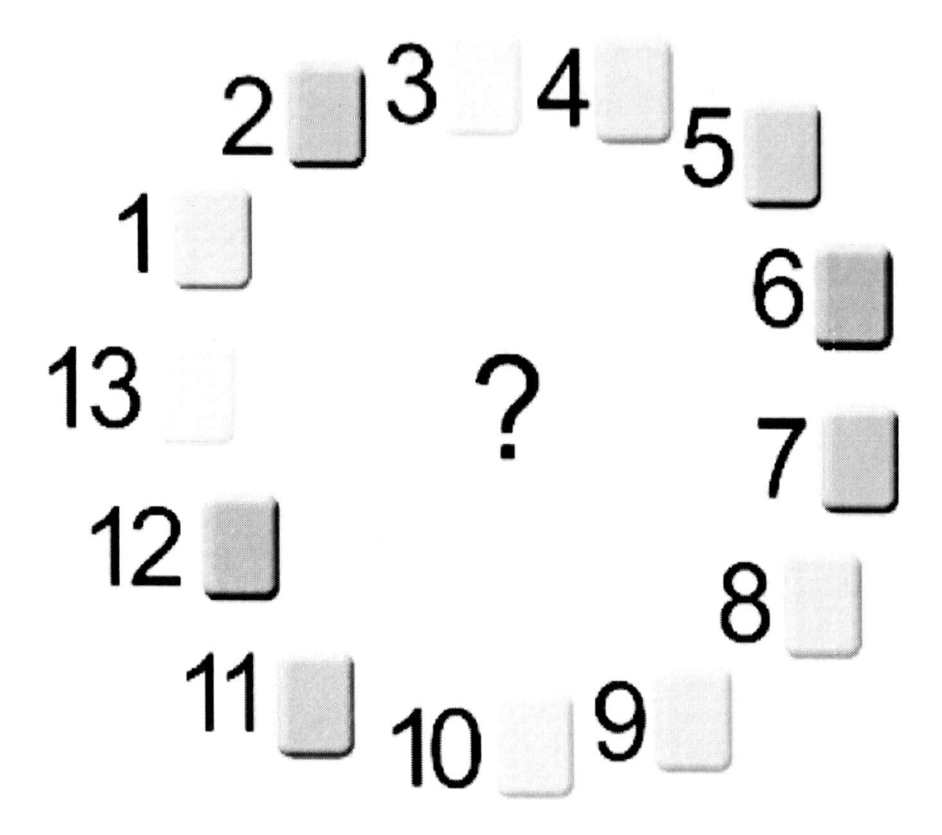

1. *Aries – Seeds, new beginnings, inspiration, new projects, birth.*
2. *Taurus – Earthly success, material wealth, physical health.*
3. *Gemini – Communication, messages, information.*
4. *Cancer – Relationships with self, people, higher forces.*
5. *Leo – Art, leadership, free will.*
6. *Virgo – Study, applied learning, skills, mastery.*
7. *Libra – Harmony, balance, negotiations, resolutions.*
8. *Scorpio – Magic, philosophy, deep matters.*
9. *Ophiuchus – Healing, transformation, alchemy.*
10. *Sagittarius – Spirituality, universal consciousness.*
11. *Capricorn – Power, authority, empire building.*
12. *Aquarius – Renewal, evolution, undoing the old.*
13. *Pisces – Soul, karmic matters, far journeys.*

The Zodiac[2] spread is a good, deep analysis as you are taking the question through the "houses" with their different spheres of influence.

Remember to take your time at the end to consider the entire symbols sphere that has developed here.

---

2 I have chosen the more esoteric 13 sign "true" zodiac for this exercise rather than the more usual 12 sign one. As always, the choice which one you prefer to use is yours.

Reading Symbol Sentences

If you are looking for answers to questions, you can also read the symbols like you would read words in a sentence, one after the other, to make a cohesive and often very poetic and moving answer.

It only takes a little practice to learn to read symbol sentences.

- **Remember to ask a question first; getting an answer to some thing you don't know what the question was is one of the most frustrating events known to humankind!**

Here is an example of my own:

"Tell me something of practical help for me today."

The symbols are:

The message I read is:

A house organised with logic and in clarity creates the perfect space for creativity.

I take this to heart and find this a useful piece of advice because I can become very disorganised when I get involved in something and things start to pile up. This then creates confusion and makes it ever more difficult to do creative things until the space is cleared and there is literally, room again to do something else.

A useful message!

Fortune Telling By Magic Stories

The Classic Game gives a vision that is a fully fledged story; unique, original, and always most pertinent to the problem in hand.

It is so that a story contains more information, more energy, more levels and layers than any good advice or how-to instruction ever could; so giving someone a story to take away, rather than just the usual, run of the mill advice can be extremely effective.

Stories also offer a person the chance to think on it further, explore it further, and figure out for themselves, and over time, how this is important for them to know.

Simply give the instruction:

"Take me to the perfect place in time and space to get a story for (xxx)."

You can refine this further by asking,

"Take me to the perfect place in time and space to get a story for (xxx) that will help (xxx) with this particular problem/situation."

Use the Classic Game and let the story unfold, using more symbols if you get stuck to move it on.

You can discuss this story afterwards with your querent.

If your querent is interested, you can also develop a story with the querent by asking THEM once the story is underway, "What would YOU like to have happen next?" or let the querent choose the next symbol themselves to develop the story further.

Dream Interpretation By Magic Story

Fortune Tellers are often also called upon to provide the service of dream interpretation. It is notoriously difficult to know what another person's dreams might mean; but if you play it like the Classic Game and consider the dream a story, you can simply unfold it until a breakthrough in understanding is reached and the meaning of the dream becomes clear to the querent.

One of the main reasons why people need help with dream interpretation, especially of nightmares, is that they wake up in the middle of the dream and before it has a chance to finish properly. This is also why they remember it and why the dream bothers them enough to seek help with it from someone else.

Here is an example how you can finish a dream using the Classic Game and the symbols, and get to the meaning and a good resolution.

This person had had a dream of inheriting an old house. It was very beautiful, and filled with antiques that might be treasures, but it was not in good repair. As they went to explore some of the rooms on the second story, they became aware that the floor was very uneven; then there was a vibration and the whole floor started to unravel, collapse in on itself. They got very scared and awoke in the middle of the night, terrified.

Treating this dream exactly as we would the Classic Game, we can step into it and ask, "What happened next?"

The person continues the story and says they fell through the ceiling, but they weren't hurt and ran out of the building, as it was clearly unsafe and needed major repairs.

It was pointed out to the person that these realms are made from energy and they could, if they wanted to, afford the repairs to the building. They were very keen to do that, rather than to destroy the old house altogether, which was also a choice; and so all manner of spirits were invited to help re-build the old house.

As they arrived, the person recognised some of them as being relatives who had died, some of them decades ago, and then it became clear that all the spirits who had come to work on the house were all ancestors from across the ages.

As the house was being restored, the person said that they had THE most amazing sense of their own "house," their own lineage across the ages being restored; and when the house was finished, there was a party with all the spirits and it was a kind of meeting place for all the family from this ancestral line. It was brightly lit and also served now as a beacon to other spirits that were related to this family to find their way there as well and not be lost in darkness any more.

The person was very excited how their "nightmare"

had revealed itself in the end; and not much later, and seemingly quite unconnected, they started a family of their own.

SPELLS & POTIONS

Here are some example spells and potions and how they were made to illustrate how energy magic works in practise.

You are very welcome to use these examples but do remember that the best spells are the ones that come from your heart, your mind and your own soul.

Mini-Spells or Spell Chants

Mini-spells are little chants that can be done at any time. Just because they are short and to the point does NOT mean they're not useful or powerful!

Remember to evoke the energies BEHIND the words and also remember the archer so you can build up the power and then discharge the FLASH into the target to create a proper magic event that you can FEEL.

Money Spell Chant

One of my favourite money spell chants that I have used for the past 6 years and it has worked every single time.

Money in my pocket

and money in my hand

money in my home

and money in the bank

money streams towards me

like the river to the sea

it's easy and it's magical

as counting 1-2-3!

Anti-Stress Spell Chant

Breathe deeply

Breathe free

friends and guides

embrace me

wind and water

lifts me

star and sun

shine upon me.

I am free

I am free

I am free.

Spell Chant To Stop Panic In A Chaos Situation

Storms within

storms without

storms above

storms below

in my centre

always stillness

'tis my will

and it is so.

Spell Chant To Bring A New Lover

Over land,

over sea,

bring my lover here to me

I love him

he loves me

bring my lover here to me

I know him

he knows me

bring my lover here to me

This is my will,

so shall it be.

Spell Chant For Making A Protection Sphere

Angels come and spread your wings

Friends protect me from all things

Light and love and wisdom bright

holds me safe and holds me tight

Loving sphere encompass me

Tis my will, so shall it be.

Spell Chant For Starting A New Project

Powers that be, hear me, see me,

guide my hand, and stand beside me

stand behind me, guide my eyes

make me true and make me wise

power and light flow through me

guide my path, so shall it be.

Spell Singing

Spells can be most intriguing when they are SUNG rather than just spoken. What do you think hymns are, at the end of the day? ☺

Now, writing your own spell song can be daunting. But you don't have to. You can

RE-WRITE a folk song or a pop song to have the right energy for what you want, what you desire.

Singing such a song when you need it is old, powerful and very natural magic indeed.

If you then add movement and dance the song at the same time as you sing it, the energies you can raise that way can be immensely powerful.

As a simple example, here is a little spell song to the tune of "Row, Row, Row Your Boat."

Fly, fly, fly so high

soar up to the sky

lifted by the winds of fate

blessed and loved am I.

Take a moment and make a spell song of your own, a little one just like this one, going for a target that you find attractive, and try it out. It's a great thing to have with you and to hum or sing or sing and dance to yourself when you need a lift, extra energy, luck or to call any form of good energy into your life you might need in the course of your day.

Potions

Potions are interesting because they are essentially bottled energy forms that are transferred to another person who will ingest them, and make them a part of their own structure in doing so, whether they want to, or not.

In that way, magic can be transferred to non-magical people and also to animals and even landscapes; and potions can be exchanged among magicians because as always, it isn't the easiest thing in the world to make your own potions, especially for certain topic matters where you have been at war with yourself, possibly for decades.

Please note that for a true magic potion, the ingredients act MAGICALLY, not chemically; so do make a distinction between let's say water with added Belladonna or Strychnine, which is a material mix, and water which has been imprinted with Belladonna and Strychnine, which is an energetic mix and what we call an energy magic potion.

Herbalism is a fascinating field in its own right and it is often mixed up with magic; but herb lore about "eating" herbs is not a magical concern, and although a magician might make it their business to study herb lore and/or chemistry to mix material potions with added magical properties as well, it is not necessary for an energy magician to do that as we are working with the energetic properties of things instead.

- **In that way, an energy magician has at their fingertips all and every substance known and quite a few that might well be entirely unknown in the hard as yet and can mix and match them to their heart's content, without ever having to worry about poisoning someone by accident, or causing havoc with the medication a person is already taking.**

In that spirit, here are some examples of energy magic potions and how to make them.

A Potion For Family Prosperity

The target: Make a prosperity potion for a family to take so that all of them move onto a new level of prosperity together and in harmony.

Finding the ingredients: Using the symbols, the Plant, the Crystal, the Artefact, the Dance, the Star and the Angel wanted to be involved.

Upon questioning the plant it came to attention that this was an Irish family and a four leaf clover should be a part of the potion. For the crystal, clear quartz was being asked for. For the Artefact, an old coin that had copper in it. For the Dance, a vibration of music and party spirit, people celebrating togetherness; it was decided to make the base with a little beer. For the Star, a blessing of love, naming all the family members and inscribing their names on a piece of paper, linking them all up in a circle. For the Angel, the Guardian Angel of the family was asked to attend for a special blessing.

The person who made this potion decided to not use any physical ingredients but to evoke the energy form of each one instead, and use a bottle of beer as the potion carrier in a symbol circle, evoking one energy form after the other, then activating the whole spell on the Star symbol.

They said that they had all through this spell a really strong sense that the ancestors of this family were very present; there was certainly a touch of the "luck of the Irish" in this potion, a willingness for hard work that gets big rewards in the end, and the best part was when the star joined up all the various family members and the whole thing catalysed explosively.

The beer bottle was duly passed to the family and each took a turn, including the children, to take a small sip of it; the rest was poured on the grounds of the family home's garden with gratitude being given to the powers that be.

A Potion For A Sad Horse

The target: A potion for a rescued horse that seems "heartbroken" and has lost the will to live, is not getting better in spite of lots of good physical care and love offered.

Finding the ingredients: The Plant symbol literally jumped out of the set, and without any further ado, a vision unfolded of freedom, green grass as wide as the eyes can see, blue skies and just being allowed to be an animal, and not having to carry any other burdens than that.

The person who made this potion had to stop and do the "clearing the paths" exercise at this point because they said they were getting very emotional. When they felt clear again, they added the following for ingredients:

Star Dust for unlimited potential for restoration and the life force that exists in everyone who is still alive; the Animal symbol for the life force of animals; the People symbol for healing the wounds people have inflicted, and the Fountain for a renewed love of life.

In this case the person decided to use real grass from their best pasture for the potion; and water from a spring on the property for the Fountain. They evoked the energy of Star Dust and welcomed the horse in the name of the other horses on the farm under the Animal symbol. For the people symbol they used their own love to catalyse the potion.

The eventual potion was made from the spring water, containing three blades of grass as physical structures in a blue glass bottle and charged in the symbol sphere.

The horse was given three drops until it was all gone and from the first time the potion was added to their drinking water, started on a remarkable road of recovery.

A Potion To Re-Awaken Interest In A Husband

The target: To re-awaken romantic interest in a husband of ten years in a wife who appears bored and dissatisfied with him.

The ingredients: the Fountain, the Trade, the Star, Star Dust, DragonWings, the Plant.

The base for the potion was to be sparkling wine, to be served to the wife at a romantic dinner at home on the anniversary of their marriage.

The other ingredients were all energetic, apart from the Plant which would be represented both energetically and physically by placing a single petal of a dark pink rose into her glass.

The bottle of sparkling wine provided by the husband was placed into the symbol circle and charged with the energies.

The person who made this potion commented that the DragonWings symbol was pivotal to the potion, to alert the wife to the presence of more levels and layers to her husband, unexplored dimensions of which she should catch a glimpse, to make her excited about knowing him more deeply and changing her mind about thinking her husband as boring and predictable.

It is reported by the husband that the potion worked "even better than I had hoped for".

SPELLS & RITUALS

Stone & Sea

On any stony shore of any ocean, or in a suitable world from the Classic Game find a private spot.

Look at the sea, tune into its grandeur and magnificence, its age and wisdom and say:

"Ocean of life, ancient sea,

take what I will give to thee."

Wait until you have aligned yourself with the vastness and infinite potential of the oceans to clean and recharge, to change and to make whole, then pick up the first stone (let yourself be guided to which one wants to help you with this specific thing).

Hold the stone in your hands, close your eyes and let "all that" flow from wherever it is stored within you into the stone and don't stop until it is all gone from you and all inside the stone.

Then step to the water's edge and say,

"Ocean of life, ancient sea,

I am giving this (person, heartache, illness, problem, old decision, bad habit et al) to thee.

Take it away from me and the land,

With your power to turn the mountains to sand.

Ocean of life, ancient sea,

I am giving this to thee

Take it away from the land and me

Take it now and I am free,

This is my will, so shall it be."

Then you take a deep breath, and throw the stone into the water.

Bow to the ancient ocean, then turn and walk away immediately.

- **This spell comes directly from a flash vision of a woman standing by the shores of the ocean, throwing her heartache and sadness away. And the flash vision arose in response to the question of, "How can I get rid of this responsibility for X which is like a stone around my neck?"**

A Simple Deliverance Spell

This is a very nice, powerful yet simple ritual to put the past behind you and get a fresh start. It was originally created for someone who wanted to get back with their husband after having treated him badly, but this basic ritual is very easily adjusted to cover "a multitude of sins" of all kinds.

Get some nice paper and a meaningful pen and ink and a fire proof dish.

Place three white candles in a triangle with the tip pointing away from you.

Light the candles and say,

"I will undo the past this night,

so that the future may be bright."

... for each one.

Cut the paper into small bits and on each one, write a short description of what exactly you did to hurt him, the "crime", if you will.

Like, "I slept with his best friend Bob," or, "I laughed behind his back," etc.

Keep doing this until each one of your "crimes" have been written down. It doesn't matter if they were little or large, but it does matter TO BE BRUTALLY HONEST JUST THIS ONCE and to get it all out.

When you have them all on separate little pieces of paper, you take three deep breaths and say,

"I accept what I did do,

now I move forward to the new."

... and burn the first one.

For each one you burn, you say the same thing again until you have only a bowl full of ashes. As this spell progresses, you will feel relief building up, and at the same time, the energy that was trapped in the recrimination and shame and guilt starting to release and will power you up, and up as you go along.

When all has been burned, stand up and focus on your new self, a wiser person, a person who is less angry and sad, more compassionate and powerful, and who has thoroughly learned from their mistakes.

Take all that energy you have raised and say,

"The price is paid, the lessons learned

A better me for which I yearned

Has come to pass, I'm on my way

This is my will, this is my say.

The new has begun,

my will shall be done."

On "done" let all the energy flash from you and light up the new you in an explosion of light.

Let the after-effects ripple away; when you are ready, thank the powers that be.

Extinguish the candles, take the ashes outside and let them be blown away by the wind.

Then, just sleep.

In the morning, things will be very different.

An Easy Distance Healing Spell

Here is an excellent example of using "the magic of the moment" for good effect and letting a simple but extremely profound healing spell arise in which everyone could take part.

A friend visited us and told us he was worried about his father who had contracted pneumonia and was very ill.

Without thinking about it, I took a blue agate from the window sill. It was very cold in my hand, unusually so, and I said, "We'll dedicate this stone to be your father and thus send him some healing."

I held the stone between the palms of both hands to make the connection to this gentleman I've never met, gave my healing and support intention, then passed the stone to the next person in the group.

Everyone took a turn, even the children present. No-one asked or needed to ask what they were supposed to do; the stone made it easy and completely natural to focus their prayer for his well being. Each person did it fast and with high intensity, which is what works the best and it did not take very long at all.

When the stone came back to me, I sealed the healing intentions and then made a little comfortable nest for the stone from a tiny bowl with some cotton wool in which I placed it on the household altar.

And that was that. We got on with what we were doing.

Three days later, I passed the altar in the afternoon and got a clear message that the stone had finished its task. I took it from its nest, send a final blessing to the unknown gentleman far away, cleared the stone and put it back where it had originally come from.

This is extremely easy, immensely natural and the whole thing just flowed, completely integrated into the general activities and I believe that is exactly how magic should be - a part of our every day life and something you just do when you're called upon to do it.

Safe Revenge Spell

What do we do when someone has hurt us and we want to get them back?

Turn to the dark side and become evil ourselves? Become no better than those perpetrators?

Surely, there must be a better way ... and there is!

This spell was shown to me by one of my guides, exactly as it stands, and it works a treat.

Here is how to do it.

Consider the person in question, and especially their shortcomings in totality.

Now consider their higher self as well, and how they are totally failing to living up to being anything like that.

Now, choose a POSITIVE QUALITY that if it was bestowed on this person, would create maximum conflict, chaos and disruption in their lives.

For example, a vicious drug dealer who exploits people would have a really hard time of it if they were to develop a conscience, all of a sudden. Or if their heart was to open to love and understanding, or if they were to develop deep insight into how their actions affect others, or how what they're doing is against the grace of the Creative Order.

For such a person, just about any positive quality, such

as:

- honour
- love
- freedom
- vision
- understanding
- clarity
- intelligence
- heart & soul opening
- connecting to higher spiritual sources
- enlightenment

... etc. would cause a real "crash and burn" in their current activities/incarnational unfoldments.

Their "muppet identity" would fall apart and they would suffer GREATLY in the process.

You, on the other hand, if you were to get these positive qualities rebound back upon you, will stand to GAIN greatly.

You stand to profit thrice -

Firstly, you get your revenge and suffering payback on the muppet level;

Secondly, you get to do "the right thing" in consultation with their higher selves;

Thirdly, YOU get back what YOU send out threefold as a bonus and as this is a positive quality you are sending, something to really look forward to!

Ready?

Light a single, simple candle and sit before it.

Call up the person's higher self (by going to a perfect place in time and space where you can meet with them).

Ask the higher self for one or more quality which would derail that person's current life and which they would not just allow you to bestow upon their charge, but actively help and encourage you to send to them on this occasion.

Thank the higher self and return to the room with the candle flame.

Now, see the actual person as they are and name these new qualities to gift them to the person:

Upon the planes in which I live,

the gift of [insert quality] I now give,

to [insert name of revenge target] with all my heart and soul,

to change [him/her] and to make [him/her] whole;

By all on high and law of three,

this is my will, so shall it be.

Visualise the person strongly in the candle flame as you are blasting them with this energy, then blow out the candle.

It is done.

- **When people really upset me these days, I have a little saying I might tell them or send them in an email which captures the spirit of this spell quite nicely:**

"I have been in touch with your higher self, and you will be hearing from it shortly."

Butterfly Spell For A New Future

Sometimes, you come to the end of an "in life incarnation". You know you can't go on like you used to, and a major transformation is required now. What used to be comforting and good has run its course, and that could be a job, a relationship, where you live, or all of it at the same time, and CHANGE is what needs to happen.

This "Butterfly" spell calls on the fascinating power of metamorphosis and calls new opportunities for a complete life transformation into your unfoldments.

Draw a butterfly shape on a piece of paper, colour it and cut it out.

That is going to be the symbol for the new life that is awaiting you and the transformation you have to undergo to step into your new life.

By all means, spend some time doing this and do it with love, and think about the colours as you do it - golden sunshine over new shores, luscious green of health and wealth, blue like the eternal oceans, red like roses of love, purple for delicious magic and so forth.

Place your butterfly into the centre of a table and get your symbols out, to form a complete symbol sphere around the butterfly.

For each symbol that you pick, choose a quality to help define your new future.

For example, on the House symbol you might state a house that you love and that loves you back; on the Crystal symbol a new clarity like you've never known before; on the people symbol contemplate the kind of people the new incarnation would bring with them into your life, and so forth.

When the symbol is complete, discharge the entire power of the symbol sphere and the powers that be into the butterfly.

For the very last step, burn the butterfly to set the magic free and put it completely into the hands of the powers that be from that moment forth.

ENERGY CREATIONS

One of the most fabulous and exciting aspects of energy magic is our ability to create energy objects at will.

We have already come across the idea of making energy magic charms, and also the Art Solutions energy magic paintings; but a true energy creation simply exists on the level of energy, and remains otherwise invisible.

There is no end to what you can do with energy creations, and the more you do this, the more profound and effective these things made from "nothing but energy" become.

These energy creations can be installations, such as fountains, waterfalls, protective and warming fires, invisible crystals, invisible house plants and more; but they can also be energy pets, such as little dragons (or large dragons!) you can call upon to entertain you, or protect you, or any form of spirit animal.

Finally there are those occurrences that I would not call strictly an energy creation, but more of an energy evocation, such as friends which can and will manifest to such a degree that others who are switched on can clearly perceive them in the room, and describe them to a T.

The world of energy magic creations is fantastic, truly exciting and can make the most tedious of environments into – well anything you could ever want them to be!

Let's start with a personal safety energy creation, one of my favourites.

Riversmooth Shield & Glamour

The Riversmooth glamour is a way to shape your aura so it becomes a flowing mirror that takes attention which comes your way and flows it away and around you, so you simply don't show up on their radar - you disappear. At the same time, it is perfectly clear from within, so it isn't a shield that stops you from seeing/experiencing what's going on around you which I think is very important as well.

You need to practise this daily both in and out of the actual stress situations to get good at it, but it is very simple and natural and you'll get the hang of it quickly.

In essence, you evoke (not imagine, EVOKE!) a protective shell around you, like an egg that encases you completely.

The outside of this egg is "riversmooth" - flowing, and it reflects back whatever comes your way, but at the same time, also carries it away, like a river would.

The great advantage of this is that you are safe inside, but also that the people who talk to you and look at you from the outside don't really feel as though you are putting up barriers or that you are blocking them, because their energies do get taken away and that gives them a sense of relief.

Keep your elbows close to your sides and extend your lower arms and hands. Palms open, pointing upwards.

Breathe deeply a couple of times, focus and say clearly, "I evoke Riversmooth" and let energy stream from your hands, create the bubble all around you, and into the ground as well below your feet.

The first few times you do this, take your time; remember that this bubble doesn't need to be very thick to work, but that it must flow (like you can see on a soap bubble).

Establish the Riversmooth shield and then practise holding it, even when your hands aren't in the position where you created it. This becomes MUCH easier with practise and it's a lifetime's skill, well, well worth learning and spending some time to perfect.

Hold it for a while, then say out aloud, "Riversmooth, dissolve." If the bubble doesn't disappear right away, use your hands to disseminate it (like waving smoke away). This too becomes easier and quicker with practise.

Riversmooth is as close to a real "invisibility spell" as you can get; when you get good at it, you can use it for all sorts of things and including to project glamours, i.e. appearing to others in a different way than you really are (younger, older, more or less authoritative, belonging, standing out as special, drawing one person's attention or everyone's, and even having people seeing things that aren't there at all, such as a different eye colour, hair colour, size, clothes and even race and gender).

As with all things, practice makes perfect and it is only in the doing of it that you get better at it.

I consider this to be one of the most practically useful types of magic in the world of non-magical people for many reasons, safety being amongst the most important, so I recommend this highly.

Energy Artefacts

One of the most wonderful things about working with energetic realities in preference is that you can have ANY OBJECT, any artefact, anything at all in space and time that ever existed or will ever exist, to enjoy, to play with, to use – and it doesn't cost a single penny.

Creating energy artefacts at will is like all things to do with magic a skill that gets better with practice; and all the rules for energy objects apply and work the same way as we have discussed throughout.

The better you get at directing your attention and shaping energy forms so they become more and more steady, resonant and REAL in every sense of the word, the more fun you have and the better this works.

Even with absolute beginners however, it is right away something you can FEEL – and that's more than good enough to get you started.

Here are some examples of simple, practical energy artefacts.

The Snow Globe

The Snow Globe is a kind of energetic multi-purpose crystal ball in which you can put things, energy forms, to transfer them, get rid of them, pass them over to the powers that be, and much more besides.

Simply begin to form an energy field between your hands; shape it as though you were making a sculpture with your hands, and with your intention begin to see the snow globe happening as you do so.

Keep it up until it becomes so real, you can feel it tingling right through your body; you can then carefully let go off it and it will float quite happily in front of you.

You can use this snow globe as a crystal ball to show you things; but also as container and that has many applications.

One is to put disturbing thoughtfields, energy fields that contain disturbing information, images, feelings and so forth into the snow globe, and the handing the whole thing over to the powers that be to do something with it.

This is a very powerful process which often leads to not just "getting rid" of disturbances; but to get feedback, or a cleaned and cleared version coming back to you later.

I have often used this method to transfer people that were giving me trouble to the powers that be for processing, as I wasn't sure I would be doing right by them or me, especially if they hurt me a lot. Simply put the person and all that pertains to them, all the bad memories, feelings and ideas, into the globe and hand it over, and that's that. Phew!

The Owl Feather

The owl feather is an example of a useful energy artefact for use in healing but this extends to all sorts of other applications.

I was doing some hands on healing and wasn't getting through – I wasn't getting the right vibration. I asked for assistance, and an owl feather materialised in my hand. I used it to stroke that person's injury and it responded immediately to the touch.

Once you have played the Classic Game for a few times, and worked with the symbols for a while, it really is as simply as to ask, "Give me something that will work, right here, right now!" and to be able to rely upon the fact that the right object will materialise.

This is a form of our old friend, The Gift; only here, we are holding it in our hands and using it as a tool to shape reality.

Silk Scarves & Cloaks

A class of very useful energy objects is clothing related – silk scarves of many colours, according to what you need at the time, and cloaks for those more heavy duty moments and happenings, are just as example.

As a simple example, let a silk scarf come to you now, of the right colour, of the right size, and put it about your shoulders right now; let it enfold you, enrich you, protect you, simply sit back and enjoy this energy form that came to you so freely, so readily.

There isn't a hard cloak on Earth, no matter how expensive, rare or otherwise imbued that can begin to compete with a cloak woven from pure rainbows; from the cleansing rain; from the rising sun or from the starry night sky; from the ocean blue or the sky high; from the mists over the moors or from the tropical rain forest in all its life and splendour.

All these things are THERE for you to use, to make your own, to dance with, to delight in and to have at any time you want. It's quite extraordinary really.

We are indeed, blessed.

Energy Installations – Home & Garden

Every house has by virtue of being in the same place for a long time, certain places where energetic rubbish accumulates over time; and some houses are not in the most helpful of natural environmental occurrences.

You can totally transform the energy of your house and every room with energy installations.

For example, in a house where there was a constant in-and-out of all sorts of people, all bringing their various gremlins and disturbances with them, the owner installed a magic shower in the main doorway that would basically "sterilise" people's energy fields before entering, much as you have showers in public baths!

To install such a shower is as simple as holding the intention of that rushing, clearing energy curtain and to evoke it strongly and powerfully with a FLASH! so it is activated and remains standing. If it is done properly, it will last until the end of days and never needs renewing.

In another house there was "a darkness in the hallway". The energy magician the owner called in installed three energy lights of three different colours – white, pink, and green – to light up that darkness and essentially, banish it. The owner said later that they then could reduce the light bulb they used on that part of the stairs from 100 watts, which still seemed dim and dingy somehow, to a 30 watt nightlight bulb which was more than bright enough to light the way. Energy is an amazing thing ...

One person reported that they had a vortex in their kitchen, in the corner where the washing machine stood, and rubbish accumulated in that corner to an extraordinary degree, when the rest of the house was quite tidy. They felt that there was something in the underlying energy of that corner that got strengthened by the action of the washing machine which made it worse; so they put a shield in front of the washing machine to keep the vortex confined behind it. The corner ceased being untidy immediately and stayed clean after that was done.

During the re-modelling of my house, I had to stay in rented accommodation and my sound equipment ended up through lack of space in my bedroom. There was a lot of stuff – keyboards, numerous computers, sound cards, instruments, microphones, amps, speakers, miles of cabling and all sorts that created some kind of major energetic noise which stopped me from going to sleep at night, even when everything was unplugged completely and technically and electrically "quiet".

I placed a tropical waterfall between the sound equipment and my bed which completely countered the noise from the equipment and was incredibly soothing (and refreshing!) to go to sleep with. I didn't take it down when I moved back so it's probably still there – I hope the current residents find it likewise amusing and helpful!

Many people would like to have fairies visit their garden.

One energy magician made this happen by creating an invisible fairy space featuring a lovely energy fountain with particularly sweet water in a nice sun-blessed spot. There they made offerings of The Gifts for the fairies on a regular basis. Not much later, they reported making contact with the Fairy kingdom in a new way and learning many new things about their forms and ways of magic.

As an exercise, when you next get up and move about your space – your home or your place of work – pay some attention to spaces that feel draining, neglected, sad, sick, poor or miserable and let an idea for a nice energy installation come to you.

Also, when you are out and about, take notice and by all means, put such installations into public spaces such as town squares, town halls, schools, and hospitals, to mention but a few.

It is definitely the cheapest and most effective way to transform your environment – and good practice, AND a whole lot of fun.

Energy Pets & Invisible Friends

If you have ever known a child who had a real invisible friend, or you were such a child once, then you will have some understanding of just how real such invisible friends can become.

Energy pets and invisible friends have innumerable uses; here are just some examples to get you going.

Toy Poodle

There was a lady who had been under a lot of stress at work and started to have panic attacks, especially when forced to cross streets with busy traffic of cars and buses.

Whilst working with an energy magician, she remembered a toy poodle made from white wool she had when she was a child and which had been a source of great comfort to her.

This white poodle was brought forward and across as an energetic reality, as an energy pet that could be with her as she was walking by the busy streets and crossing them too; a most helpful helper, friend and reminder for this lady which significantly changed her experience of going to work for the better.

Energy Familiars

Energy only familiars are an amazing occurrence in their own right. As a child, there was a spirit horse that used to visit me, and on at least one occasion actually saved my life. A spirit dog saved my son's life when he was very small by alerting me to the fact that he had fallen into a pond and was drowning.

I know a person who has a spirit cat, a dearly beloved familiar which passed to the spirit world some decades ago but is so very present, I can see it in the room, and I can hear it too, as can other people apart from the owner. This spirit animal has helped the person over the years in innumerable ways, also saving their life on a number of occasions and giving heed and warning when things are wrong.

There was one occasion where a con man worked his way down the whole street in the neighbourhood, and everyone believed him and gave him money for a community project; but the spirit cat hissed when the person opened the door to him so they were not fooled; they were the only ones to refuse and send him away empty handed.

At first, the neighbourhood spat at the person for being selfish and not wanting to contribute to the good of the community; when the scam was revealed, this was replaced with a level of reverence and the person is now often consulted on important subjects by individuals, as well as by the community leaders.

The moral of these stories is that energy familiars are a HUGE resource; and the more attention you give them, the more you interact with them, and the more that you can simply accept them for being quite real, and being here, the more they can do for you in return.

And that includes most definitely, saving your life and that of your loved ones.

The Wits

At one point I noted the saying, "I have my wits about me," and started to muse what these wits might be. I saw them as white creatures, like birds or more likely, miniature dragons, each one intelligent in its own right and useful to me, and all together a real source of power, information, wisdom and steadiness.

Some of us may have "lost their wits" at some point, and some may have gone astray; calling back all your wits to you and if any are stuck anywhere, have friends or other wits help to find them and guide them home, is clearly a good idea. ☺

Since then, quite a few people have made friends with their wits and use them to be posted as guards in dangerous situations; occupy seats on buses, planes and in theatres if they didn't want someone to sit on them; guard children; sent them out to gather information and bring it back; and to come in close when you really "need your wits about you" to solve problems or get yourself out of tricky situations. Wits can also mount an attack, "The Birds" style, if all else fails, and drive people and entities away that you don't want anything to do with.

Interesting and well worth having a look at.

Friends

The most useful energy helpers overall are of course, the friends.

That is the global word we use for helpful entities and includes spirit guides but also all sorts of other beings that you meet along the way.

Most people don't use a single percent of the potential that friends bring with them and simply don't give them enough love and attention to ENABLE them to become more powerful, and thereby, more practically useful to you.

We have mentioned the strength of the reality of an energetic being that is really being accepted for what it is, loved and cared for, and most of all INCLUDED in your daily life and business a few times before; here is one more time to remind us all again that especially our best spirit friends DESERVE much more than we are giving them.

Here are my top tips for activating your friends (guides) to a much higher level.

1. Care enough to ask them questions and find out more about them! Don't just be "me me me" when it comes to dealing with your spiritual advisors!

2. Invite them into your house, into your home. Include them in your life, invite them to your party, make them a spot in your home and

garden where they are always welcome. Share your embarrassing secrets with them, show them how hard your life can be, how you are not perfect, WHAT your challenges are, what your faults and failings are, perceived and otherwise. ONLY IF THEY REALLY KNOW YOU can they REALLY HELP YOU.

3. Do not be overly respectful of "Chief Running Elk" or his kind. He was a man (or some kind of being in the hard) at some point. He went to the toilet. He liked to lick honey off a spoon. He had a favourite blanket he used to call "my snuggly" when nobody was looking. Get to know him! Let him be REAL. Give him permission to be real rather than some spooky icon and he will repay you with REAL magic he can do on your behalf.

That last point is really OF THE ESSENCE when we talk about getting REAL, powerful help from friends.

- **The more real you can allow your friends to become, the more real the effects they have – a simple cause and effect.**

By paying attention to them, by loving them, you empower them. It is so simple, and it works so well, and it works for all and every entity because the Universe itself is made from love, and runs on love as its fuel and actual currency. As you learn more about love, and become likewise more empowered and have more love to give, you can have more relationships with more loved, empowered beings.

Friends can be fairies, alien entities, and also the much maligned "hitchhikers" who quite literally are disembodied spirits that hitch a ride on other living beings' incarnations.

Hitchhikers

I come from a culture where people are accepted for what or who they are without asking too many questions; where strangers are treated well in principle; and where everyone has to pull their weight for the good of the community.

So instead of going nuts with terror when discovering I had some hitchhikers on board and going all out to destroy them, cut them off or cast them out, I thought I would welcome them instead, find out more about them and see if they could make themselves useful.

That was the right decision.

The hitchhikers became good friends, were absolutely delighted to not have been rejected or to spend their astral journey with me in terror of being discovered and cast into the lightless void; they have proved themselves to be a major asset on **my** journey. They are a part of my crew and I love them dearly. I am also glad that I can be of service in this way by providing a safe haven and a safe step on their evolution, unfoldment and path.

Should I ever become a disembodied spirit, I would sincerely hope that someone else would take me in and treat me right, that's for sure!

And now for a very "special" class of entities that might come in handy one day ...

The Specialists

Sometimes, you need a specialist for a special job.

In the days of medieval madness, it was held to be a good idea to capture a vicious demon and "make them" act on your behalf, to win a court case, for example, or influence an election or such.

Most of the time, I do believe these lunatics didn't actually capture anything, they made the demon themselves in crazy blood soaked rituals that went on for days on end, constructing it out of their own distorted thoughtfields and terrors. And they built into this horror construct the fact that it would hate them, hate to work for them, and bite them in the arse, given the first opportunity or moment of weakness by their so called "master"!

Good God!

I've met a few entities that might be called "a demon" if you were to look through that strange distortion glass of medieval madness ("Where even the most beautiful landscape would look like boiled spinach!") but I prefer to call entities instead.

I can tell you with some authority that these things have really NO interest in your court cases, divorces or elections; and to get them to do something about that would be like trying to train a very large feral tiger to water sky.

What is the point of that?

What we do in energy magic instead is to find entities that are

A. **right for the job; and**

B. **willing to do it.**

I call these **"The Specialists"**.

How do you find a specialist for a particular job?

"Show me to the perfect place in time and space where I can meet a specialist who can make X happen."

Remember your "clearing the paths" exercise when you go to meet specialists; because they are often strange, unusual and may cause a fear response if you are not used to dealing with very alien entities.

You can trust in the fact that your higher self, and your supporting crew, and your powers that be would NOT and NEVER take you to meet a specialist who would do you harm. That's the beauty of the Classic Game – you get taken to THE RIGHT specialist for the job.

However, there is certainly a measure of people skills required in dealing with a specialist; those are the same skills for hiring help anywhere. Don't be an idiot, disrespect the specialist and throw your weight around; and don't be a push over and let them walk all over you – it's the same for tradesmen and specialists the world over.

Agree a payment with them and make sure you instruct them correctly and to the degree that they really know what they are supposed to be doing. That's exactly like hiring builders, or accountants, or an interior designer – if you are not exact and specific, they do as they please or try and guess, and the outcome is usually a huge argument, and a lot of unnecessary negativity.

If you find that all very daunting, simply take a friend or two to help you negotiate a good deal with the specialist.

The specialist will then go into action and do what the deal decreed; and we have our outcome, without any trouble or having to spill any goats' blood whatsoever.

Simples!

FAREWELL ...

And so, we come to the end of this introduction to modern energy magic, spells, and potions.

In this book, I have wanted to give you a pathway to real magic that is based on the living Universe and us people being a full and welcome part and participant of the same.

With the principles of how energy works, the Classic Game and The Genius Symbols, you have a tool set that you can literally spend a lifetime exploring, and never get tired of it, never get to the end of, that will grow with you, support you unconditionally on your own highest path - and have exciting and fun experiences along the way.

We people are magical by nature, and we are designed to stretch and reach, flex our wings and grow towards the sky in a very real sense.

When you light up the magic in your life, things can never be the same.

The more you enjoy it, the more you step into it, and the more you ALLOW YOURSELF to find love, treasures, riches, fabulous energies of all kinds, the more will come to you.

There is so much support for us out there, so much help, so much positive attention and so much will and hope for us to succeed in being normal, happy, healthy people who have lived wonder-filled lives on the beautiful planet of ours.

Magic is a way to realise that, to find out who we really are, and most of all, to celebrate the true wonder that is life, the Universe and everything in it – unconditionally so.

I wish you much joy, gifts and surprises on your perfect path and I bless you not once, not twice, but thrice with all my heart,

StarFields

aka

Dr Silvia Hartmann

June 21st, 2009

FURTHER READING...

The Patterns & Techniques of EmoTrance by Silvia Hartmann

Oceans of Energy: The Patterns & Techniques of EmoTrance Volume 1

EmoTrance is a new system for handling the human energy body. 'Oceans of Energy' gives a thorough grounding in the underlying principles of EmoTrance™ for self help and use with others and introduces the uses of the system, namely self healing, healing others, goal setting, and state management, especially of new and previously unexperienced enlightenment states. Includes discussion of the developmental history of the system, stories from practitioners and first person reports of EmoTrance in the field.

Living Energy: The Patterns & Techniques of EmoTrance Volume 2

In November 2003, sixty top EmoTrance Trainers and Practitioners came together in Eastbourne, United Kingdom, to find out about the latest techniques, patterns and exercises from the EmoTrance Universe. This book contains a full and uncensored transcript of everything which transpired during those two days, plus extensive supporting addendi.

Energy Magic: The Patterns & Techniques of EmoTrance Volume 3

This is the third and final part of the EmoTrance Energy series, and this book concerns itself with what happens when healing has been accomplished, and we cast our intentions and minds to what we should be doing next.

EmoTrance Energy Dancing by Silvia Hartmann

Energy Dancing I: Energy Self Healing Through Movement & Music

Energy Dancing is a completely natural and intuitive way to increase energy flow throughout the body. This causes emotions to change for the better, as well as being a very fast method to de-stress and re-energize profoundly, in under five minutes.

Energy Dancing II: The Sacred Horse by Silvia Hartmann

Experience profound relief, release, de-stress and exercise your mind, your body, your energy body with this brilliant NEW self help program from the acclaimed Energy Dancing series, created by Dr Silvia Hartmann.

Project Sanctuary & The Genius Symbols

Project Sanctuary: Mind, Energy & Metaphor Magic by Silvia Hartmann

Project Sanctuary is a unique set of processes using intention, energy and metaphor, developed by Dr Silvia Hartmann in 1993, that heals the divide between the conscious mind and the energy mind (unconscious mind, dreaming mind, subconscious mind). It is a fantastic, exciting and delightful process that every human being can engage in. "If you only buy ONE book in this lifetime - make it Project Sanctuary."

The Genius Symbols: Your Portal to Creativity, Imagination and Innovation by Silvia Hartmann

Dr Silvia Hartmann defines what it means to be a true genius and proposes that this is a basic human right, rather than an accident of birth. In this paradigm shifting work, which is the result of nearly five decades of research and testing, The Genius Symbols are introduced.

Sidereus Genius Symbols: Correspondence Training Programme

A NEW and truly exciting distance learning course that will help you improve conscious/unconscious communication IMMEASURABLY. 6 superb, information packed units and truly FASCINATING exercises will bring you a wealth of new learnings, new information, new insights and most of all, INVALUABLE experience in using YOUR systems in an entirely ecological and always surprising way.

Sidereus Project Sanctuary: Correspondence Training Programme

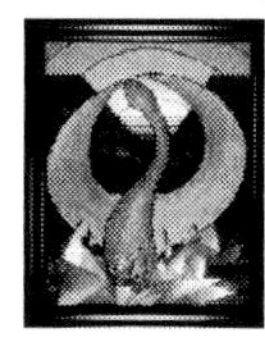

The Project Sanctuary distance learning course, written researched and developed by Dr Silvia Hartmann, PhD. Project Sanctuary has been widely hailed as one of the most exciting contributions to our understanding of unconscious / conscious communications. The greatest poetry, stories, scientific discoveries and works of art have all come from a place of creativity way beyond what can be achieved by working exclusively in the consciousness. Even Einstein discovered relativity by "riding on a beam of light"! So how do you learn to tap into your most creative resource? How can you possibly learn to become a genius who can tap into their own creativity at will? Available with or without tutor support.

The Soul Pilots: Service Has Its Own Rewards by Silvia Hartmann et al

The Soul Pilots is an enchanting collection of Soul Pilotting stories written down by seven Project Sanctuary Masters and collated by Project Sanctuary developer Silvia Hartmann. Each of the 76 stories is truly unique and absolutely beautiful. Read on for more information about Soul Piloting.

Far Journeys: Mind Expanding Personal Journeys by Silvia Hartmann

To the realms of Project Sanctuary comes Far Journeys by master lady hypnotist Silvia Hartmann. This CD or MP3 download set contains four superb guided energy hypnosis experiences taking you to four very different planes. Far Journeys is an infinite resource for creativity, intelligence enhancing, lucid dreaming, problem solving, spiritual growth and healing. Buy the Far Journeys today and receive the special bonus CD: The Earth Rise Visualisation Trainer double induction FREE of charge.

Fiction by StarFields

The Magician: 28 Lessons in Magic

The Magician is a deeply moving story of one woman's journey of transformation. This extraordinary novel by master story teller Starfields engages the emotions as well as the mind and it contains sequences of events and images that will stay with the reader forever. Fascinating, surprising, and entirely delightful, The Magician is a book you will want to read again, and again.

Vampire Solstice: Love Forever ...

Fantasy Fiction by StarFields. For the Vampire community, the Solstice Choosing has been the holiest night of the year - for a hundred thousand years. But this year, something new is about to happen. The oldest prophecies are about to be fulfilled - and the Festival of Blessings is finally upon us.

The Golden Horse & Other Fairy Tales: 16 New Enchanting Tales of Mystery & Imagination For The Magical Child by Silvia Hartmann

Created by Master Story Teller Silvia Hartmann For Magical Children Aged 9 - 99, The Golden Horse is an anthology of absolutely original, highly creative stories told in traditional fairy tale format to enlighten, inspire and foster curiosity and delight in exploration. Modern yet ageless, hypnotic and enchanting, perfect for being read out and spoken aloud, these stories will speak to the magical child within us all.

In Serein: Sorcerer & Apprentice

Young commoner Isca is determined to become a Serein magician so that she may take charge of her destiny and no longer remain a victim to the circumstances of her birth and the oppressors of her world. She is apprenticed to the only master strong enough to control her, the immortal Lord Lucian Tremain, acting Lord of Darkness. In the conjunction between Lord Lucian's ancient powers and Isca's unprecedented talents, a force is born that can take the stars from the sky - but only if they can learn to survive one another. The In Serein trilogy was written between 2000 - 2001 and is Silvia Hartmann's first published major fiction project.

Improve Psychic Skills, Paranormal Abilities with Energy Hypnosis

The Appollonius Quartet by StarFields

Paranormal abilities and psychic skills arise from a co-operation between the psychic circuitry, the energy system and the active neurology. This set of tools will SIGNIFICANTLY improve all aspects of psychic and paranormal performance by removing shields and blockages in these systems, healing existing injuries and laying out a pathway for practice, new learnings and self guided explorations.

The Aromatherapy Collection

Aromatherapy For Your Soul: Creative Aromatherapy & Aromaenergy for Love, Life & Luxury by Silvia Hartmann

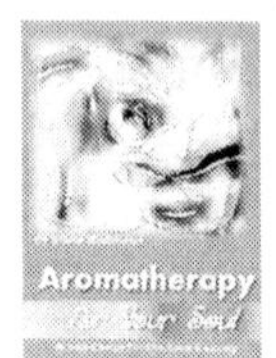

This wonderful book introduces 121 stunning Aromatherapy Essential Oils & explains their purposes for our energetic, spiritual and emotional health in a totally different way. Take your love of Aromatherapy to the next level and discover the enchanted world of Aroma Energy - Aromatherapy For YOUR Soul. Learn to use Essential Oils to fill your deepest desires, still ancient hungers and delight you, transform your daily life and bring you rich wisdom, luxury, protection and the most wonderful stimulation of all your systems. Contains beautiful images and 121 original metaphor teaching stories for all ages.

Creative Aromatherapy by Silvia Hartmann

Let aromatherapy essentials really come to life and become a powerful force of good in your incarnation! Silvia Hartmann will teach you how you can get the very best out of your own essentials with simple, easy and quick exercises that light up your energy awareness and brilliant, innovative and ingenious ways to really use essentials in a whole new way.

Magic Garden Meditation by Silvia Hartmann & Silvia Hartmann

Walk in your own enchanted, magical garden full of vibrant plants, herbs and flowers to find YOUR perfect healing plant with this BEAUTIFUL and powerful energy meditation, especially created by Dr Silvia Hartmann to help you feel, see and sense the amazing resonant energies of the plant kingdom, and to connect deeply and powerfully with the essentials themselves. A perfect quarter hour of deepest relaxation, wonderful lucid dreaming and absolutely amazing energy experiences you can access whenever YOU need a special magic plant from your very own magical garden.

HypnoDreams & Energy Hypnosis

HypnoDreams 1: Wisdom of the Water by Silvia Hartmann & Ananga Sivyer

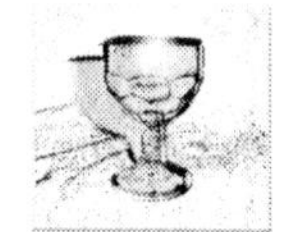

Developed in parallel with the breakthrough techniques of Energy Flow of EmoTrance, 'The Wisdom of the Water' is a fantastic collection of healing dreams, each one evoking a rich tapestry of healing energies, of states and of experiences.

HypnoDreams 2: Heart Healing by Silvia Hartmann & Ananga Sivyer

Use these powerful healing evocations to balance you, to lift you, to support you or simply as the perfect holiday in mind, body and spirit. 7 + 1 unique dreams of healing, 7 + 1 absolutely personal experiences of re-alignment and expansion. From the pure power of 'Heart Healing' to the celebration of 'The Child', we are immensely proud to present 'Heart Healing' with and by Silvia Hartmann, Ananga Sivyer and Pia.

HypnoDreams 3: Freedom by Silvia Hartmann & Ananga Sivyer

To complete this truly extraordinary trilogy, here is Freedom - powerfully uplifting, intensely inspiring and absolutely beautiful.

Past Life Regression & Beyond: Many Lives In The Multiverse by Silvia Hartmann

Past Life Regression has always been about THIS LIFE, and how other lives and their experiences are influencing what is happening FOR YOU TODAY.

In this fabulous guided energy hypnosis meditation session, Dr Hartmann takes you beyond mere "past" lives and lets you connect with ANY life that needs your attention, right here, right now:

Past lives, alternate lives, even potentially future lives can have an influence because in the quantum dimensions, ALL TIME IS AS ONE.

SuperGoals: Set A Goal - Heart & Soul!

This unique Energy Hypnosis goal setting session, created by Dr Silvia Hartmann, gets us aligned and into contact with most if not all of ourself, and from there, a new form of goal emerges - a SuperGoal, something that is truly important and agreed on by the many aspects of a person, including their heart's desires and their highest path and purpose.

Healing & Affirmations

For You, A Star: 64 POSITIVELY HEALING Energy Forms To Transform YOUR LIFE by Silvia Hartmann

In order to have good things in our lives, we need to focus on good things, drawing powerful, POSITIVELY HEALING energy forms into our lives. This outstanding book by Dr Silvia Hartmann contains 64 powerful energy evocations for mind, body and spirit - and For You A Star is as easy to use as 1, 2, 3.

Power Affirmations: 21st Century Magic Spells That Change Reality by Silvia Hartmann

In this powerful, brand new and highly focused 12 part self training program, Dr Silvia Hartmann explains exactly and concisely how you can make affirmations that work exactly like magic spells to create YOUR reality of choice. From strikingly simple exercises for absolute beginners, to the amazing Super Magic Affirmations and the Vega Pattern at the other end of the scale, this concise treaty will give you the tools to make affirmations finally come to life, and really start to WORK FOR YOU!